Future Directions in Community Power Research: A Colloquium

INSTITUTE OF GOVERNMENTAL STUDIES
UNIVERSITY OF CALIFORNIA, BERKELEY • 1971

Future Directions in
Community Power Research:
A Colloquium

FREDERICK M. WIRT, Editor
Institute of Governmental Studies
University of California, Berkeley

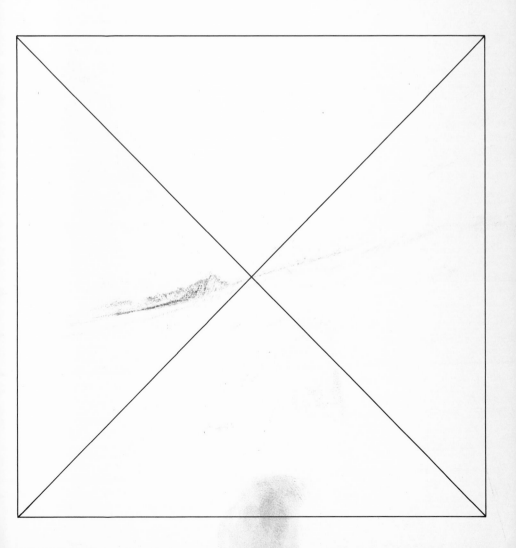

International Standard Book Number (ISBN) 0-87772-073-8
Library of Congress Catalog Card Number 78-632824
$5.00

To Jewel Prestage, whose ideas

inspired this colloquium

CONTENTS

PREFACE

In his *Politics*, Aristotle may well have made the
first study of community power in Western civilization,
for the city-states of his day had many community characteristics. His was undoubtedly the first comparative
analysis of such power systems. Indeed, at the beginning
of the study he set forth the centrality of the comparative method:

> ...governments differ in kind, as will
> be evident to anyone who considers the
> matter according to the method which
> has hitherto guided us. As in other
> departments of science, so in politics,
> the compound should always be resolved
> into the simple elements or least parts
> of the whole. We must therefore look
> at the elements of which the state is
> composed, in order that we may see in
> what the different kinds of rule differ
> from one another, and whether any scien-
> tific result can be attained about each
> one of them.

Yet almost 25 centuries elapsed between that beginning and the next serious effort in the comparative
analysis of public decisionmaking. While the Romans
incorporated laws and administrative techniques drawn
from experience with imperial conquests, no comparative
analysis has come down to us. Machiavelli might advise
his Prince by drawing upon the experience of the Renais-
sance city-states, but his preoccupation with the personal quality of powerholding precluded any community
analysis. Histories of their communities by nineteenth
century Americans and Britons abound, but the concern is
rarely for the process of local decisionmaking. Instead
they exude "boosterism" about the benevolence that God
had visited upon the locality.

Lincoln Steffens' *Shame of the Cities*, written early in this century as part of the Progressive reevaluation of the quality of American life, was a start in a new direction. This was not merely because Steffens challenged boosterism, but because he used the comparative method, albeit crudely. Even the field work of the Lynds--which was preceded, the intellectual historian should note, by novelists of the new realism--focused narrowly on one site: "Middletown" during the eras of normalcy and depression. The history of this special field of study since the Lynds--and certainly since Floyd Hunter--should be familiar to the reader and thus need not be recounted here.[1]

During the 15 years since Hunter's study of "Regional City," more research has been undertaken, more communities have been studied, and more has been learned about the structure of local decisionmaking apparatus than ever before in our history. Thus the field has contributed to the information explosion characteristic of the post-World War II period. As the reports by Floyd Hunter and Terry Clark in the present volume indicate, even the computer has appeared in this field.

Attendant upon, or contributing to, this scholarly growth has been the development of a host of conceptual, theoretical and methodological innovations. Recounting these alone would fill volumes, as witness the recently edited works by Terry Clark and Charles Bonjean.[2] The most controversial development relates to the method of

---

[1] A review of those developments is provided in Willis D. Hawley and Frederick M. Wirt, eds., *The Search for Community Power* (Englewood Cliffs, N.J.: Prentice-Hall, Inc., 1968).

[2] Terry N. Clark, ed., *Community Structure and Decision-Making: Comparative Analyses* (San Francisco: Chandler Publishing Co., 1968) and the entire issue on community politics, *Southwestern Social Science Quarterly*, 48(3) (1967), edited by Charles M. Bonjean.

finding decisionmakers, but others are equally important, if less widely discussed. Many of these questions are raised in this book, particularly in the essays by Charles Adrian and Harry Scoble.

But the methodological debate that occasioned such passionate exchanges in the political science and sociology journals during the last decade was not emphasized at the conference that produced these papers. All the participants acknowledge that the mainstream of current research embodies combinations of methods flowing from the earlier "reputational" versus "decisional" debate.

One strong current in recent research has been an increasing awareness that we must move beyond the case study and its methods of analysis to aggregate data and the distinctive methods of analysis they require. The call for comparative analysis is heard on every hand in this field; almost all the essays presented here explicitly or implicitly echo this call. John Walton lifts our sights beyond the American polity and urges the international crossbreeding of concepts, theories and methods used in research on community power, economic development and social organization. Bonjean suggests the application of previous work in individual psychology to leadership study; Adrian and Clark indicate the uses of system theory and input-output analysis; and Ross Stephens demonstrates the utility of viewing the metropolis as a grid of plural decision systems. All of these urge the need for employing comparative analysis if we are ever to develop sophisticated statements about community power.

Less unanimity has been attained in the recent scholarly debate based on concern for the quality, or representativeness, of public policy. At one level, this concern is kept ostensibly quantitative or value free: the researcher asks what kinds of policies emerge or are suppressed, given a certain kind of power structure. The essays by Bonjean and Clark are illustrative. But at another level, concern for policy has been qualitative: how representative of democratic ideals, asks the

xi

researcher, are the policy outputs of certain kinds of
power structures? Does political elitism or oligopoly
obstruct the public will? Or is apparent elitism, like
the "divinity which doth hedge in a king," limited by
secular expectations and the desires of the public?

In this debate over values, there are many whose
work is oriented to the opening lines from Books I and II
of Aristotle's *Politics*:

> Every state is a community of some
> kind, and every community is estab-
> lished with a view to some good; for
> mankind always act in order to obtain
> that which they think good.... Our
> purpose is to consider what form of
> political community is best of all
> for those who are most able to realize
> their ideal of life.... And let no one
> suppose that in seeking for [this] we
> are anxious to make a sophistical dis-
> play at any cost; we only undertake
> this inquiry because all the consti-
> tutions with which we are acquainted
> are faulty.

All contributors to this volume have something to
say on the question of values, as did most members of the
conference audience. Scoble denies all notions of value-
free research; Adrian draws distinctions on the subject;
Hunter charges that the intellectual quests of the profession of Sociology are necessarily highly normative.
Such variety of response is typical of the arguments
heard elsewhere in the social sciences on this matter.
Thus this volume does not resolve the debate over the
value orientation of community power research, nor does
it evade the relevance of the problem.

After these indications of what follows, a word is
due on the origins of this volume. It began when
Southern University's Jewel Prestage, Program Chairman

for the 1968 Southwestern Social Science Convention, suggested that I assemble a panel on community power studies. I chose the theme of the colloquium, as well as the participants, and chaired the first panel. Two meetings of the panel actually developed: one at the Dallas convention and another three days later at the University of Texas, in Austin. At the suggestion of Charles Bonjean, the University had invited us to move to Austin from Dallas to develop further ideas. At the second meeting, Terry Clark chaired the panel and presented an overview of the ideas offered earlier at Dallas. The members of this colloquium, possibly the only road show panel in history, join me in expressing gratitude to Professor Prestage for her encouragement and to the University of Texas not merely for the facilities provided, but also for generosity in supporting scholarship and, we hope, learning.

A further note concerns the form of the papers in this volume. I asked the participants to present talks that would be revised in the light of panel discussions, audience comments and their own later reflections. Like the physicist Robert Oppenheimer, they were asked "to guess at night and correct in the morning." This they did, both in preparing their formal papers and revising their informal remarks. Some incorporated casual remarks into their final papers; others at my suggestion made extensive revisions of their first papers; several others decided to publish only their oral presentations. Even though it appeared in print after the Texas conference, Clark's study of 51 communities was revised for this publication. None of the other papers has been published previously.

In addition, I have included the discussion that ensued at Dallas and Austin, both among panel members and from the audience. Our recording procedures did not enable us to catch the names of our questioners: for this, my apologies are tendered. I have edited these impromptu remarks to eliminate the errors of syntax and grammar that are normal when men think and speak quickly.

Panel members reviewed the elisions and deletions, but none of us interfered with the substance of the audience's remarks. The ideas that appeared not only add to our knowledge of community power, but also reflect the flavor of the exchange of ideas among knowledgeable and concerned scholars.

Finally--but most importantly for the growth of learning in this field--we wish to express our appreciation to Eugene C. Lee, Director of the Institute of Governmental Studies, University of California, Berkeley. It was he who saw the significance of what these discussants were attempting and supported that insight by suggesting publication under Institute auspices.

If this volume is a contribution to scholarship--as we hope it is--credit is due to all these individuals.

Frederick M. Wirt
January 1971

Introductory Remarks

by FREDERICK M. WIRT

University of California, Berkeley

All of you should be familiar with the intense intellectual debate that has surrounded the question of community power in the last 15 years. After such massive effort, it may seem disparaging for me to say that little is known about the possible variety of community power structures in the thousands of American cities. But my judgment simply reflects the implicit and explicit conclusions of the current literature.

A colleague, Willis D. Hawley, has written that further progress probably rests upon the answers to three general problems. We need to know more about (1) what we seek, (2) how we find it, and (3) how we interpret what we find. First, there has been a failure to reach consensus on what is meant by power and how to make it operational. James March's recent essay on "The Power of Power" arrives at some pessimistic conclusions about the utility of the concept, concluding that perhaps we ought to pass on to something else.[1] This definitional debate is intense and often abstruse.

The second problem is the methodological point of how we find power. In many respects, this is a more mundane question, although it has involved the resources and intellectual passions of many social scientists. Yet as the conclusions of Robert Presthus et al. show, this debate seems to be resolving itself through the use of multiple techniques for pinpointing power. There still remains the problem of how to weight and integrate the results obtained by these different measures. But much of the recent literature suggests that this general question has commanded too much of our time, and that combinations of methodologies increase our chances of mirroring the multifaceted varieties of community life.

---

[1] March, in *Varieties of Political Theory*, ed. David Easton (Englewood Cliffs, N.J.: Prentice-Hall, Inc., 1966), pp. 39-70.

The third point, how we interpret what we find, is
the concern of our panel. The central question is: How
can we develop a conceptual framework that encompasses
the seemingly disparate results the literature reveals?
Such a conceptualization and its testing require the use
of a comparative framework. John Walton, a member of
this panel, has written, "To come to grips with the
diverse social and political facets of community life in
a comparative design remains the chief problem in this
field."[2]

The problem, of course, is that for too long we have
concerned ourselves with case studies. This was necessary when resources were limited and research just beginning. Even case studies take a tremendous amount of
money, time and energy. But at the present time, there
seems to be developing a movement from individual findings to general theory, and to the testing of theory with
multiple instances. Many feel the need to escape the
"case-study" condition described by Peter H. Rossi:

> Each author owns his own town, defending
> it from the erroneous and somewhat
> heretical conceptualizations of others
> much the way a feudal lord defends the
> integrity of the local patron saint
> against the false counterclaims of
> nearby realms.[3]

What many in this area are saying, then, is that we
need to develop a comparative study of community power.
It is to this need that the present panel is dedicated.

---

[2] See Walton, "Substance and Artifact: The Current
Status of Research on Community Power Structure," *American Journal of Sociology*, 71: 430-438 (1966). See especially p. 438.

[3] See Rossi, "Power and Community Structure," *Midwest
Journal of Political Science*, 4(4): 390-401 (1960). See
especially p. 391.

The ground rules are simple. Each participant has been
asked to present informally his ideas on the theme of
comparative studies, possibly including some of his current research. Each has a maximum of 10 to 15 minutes to
present his paper, with a period for questions from the
audience. We hope this presentation will stimulate
thought among the audience as well as reformulation and
clarification of their ideas by panel members.

Several Loose Ends in Theory Building

by CHARLES R. ADRIAN
University of California, Riverside

CONTENTS

It's good to see that we have finally gotten the adversaries to the conference table. I trust that after today's session we will be able to de-escalate the struggle between political scientists and sociologists on this whole question. I have a number of things I would like to comment on very briefly. I might like to say that in my own research dealing with community power I have undertaken to use both the Dahl method and what is essentially the Hunterian method.

One of the things I am struck with is the rate of change in the concepts and perspectives used by people working in this area. As you probably know, Robert Dahl once wrote an article discussing the problems of explaining just what we mean by power.[1] After discussions about the article, he became so discouraged he decided we needed to discuss both power and influence, and therefore provided a separate definition for each. I am inclined to think that the direction of research today probably is more toward what Dahl describes in *Modern Political Analysis* as the structure of influence rather than the refinement of the concept of power.

It seems to me that there are many loose ends in the incipient theory-building we engage in today in political science and in the social sciences generally. I would like to comment a bit on some of these concepts and not deal with the much more difficult problem of method.

THE CONCEPT OF COMPETITIVENESS

If we were to look at possible further explorations into the conventional theory of community power, it seems that we would need to concentrate on the concept of competitiveness in the political power structure. In particular, this is necessary because of the recent politicization of a number of groups that were essentially apolitical in the community process of 15 to 20 years ago. We refer particularly to Negroes, of course, and to the poor of every color.

The Miller-Form technique, devised as a kind of quick journeyman's way to discover the community power structure, has much to commend it.[2] Among its merits, in addition to simplicity, is the ability to pick up the competitive elements of community power. One of the things we have not done, however, in looking at the competitive nature of power, is to decide whether we are now talking about a power structure or about an ecology of power structures that all happen to occupy the same arena, the same space, and that are brought together through some kind of negotiating process. Conventional power studies usually do not address themselves to this possibility at all. Indeed, the conventional studies, pioneered by sociologists, tended to ignore the notion, well-established in political science, that political leaders do not concentrate upon effecting their own policy preferences, but characteristically serve as brokers among conflicting interests.

THE NEED FOR COMPARISON

Another thing we have not spent much time on yet is tying together some of the recent comparative studies, works such as Banfield's study of the politics of major cities.[3] Banfield's approach did not lend itself to any attempt to correlate his findings with what we would have found if we had used a Miller-Form technique in each of the communities he studied. But it might be revealing to compare the results of two such differing techniques. It would be relatively simple and might tell us something about the degree to which we are talking about the same things in different languages.

I think, too, that there are a number of ways in which we might seek to improve the very simple and inexpensive Miller-Form technique. By only slightly expanding the interview task, for example, it would be possible to make sure that "knowledgeables" from groups with high political motivation (such as Negroes) were interviewed. Similarly, it would be possible to control for paranoiac responses by using a structured questionnaire with items designed to reveal paranoid attitudes toward leaders and leadership.

CONTROL OF THE AGENDA

One of the topics Robert Dahl was much concerned about, relative to community power and influence, was control of the agenda. It seems to me that we need to investigate how the community agenda is controlled. It may have been that in the days of the *Middletown* studies the local agenda could be unilaterally determined by a monolithic local power structure.[4] But I would suggest that since the advent of the poverty program, in particular, the expansion of some state programs, the question of controlling the agenda has become vastly more complex. All we have to do is look at the daily issues of the New York *Times* and note the struggles between Mayor Lindsay and Governor Rockefeller over the agenda for New York City.

It seems that today people at various levels of government can put an item onto the agenda. This raises interesting questions--can we really keep items off the agenda any longer? If we can't, given Dahl's emphasis on this point, then what does this imply for community power? If, when community leaders fail to act, somebody else will, is there any power left in the community?

THE CONCEPT OF POWER

Another area I think we might investigate is the whole question of power as a consumption item. In some studies, power is visualized as being inexhaustible, always instantly replenished. Yet this is an unlikely hypothesis in light of the concept of social capital long

accepted by sociologists, and in light of the theories of
riot, insurrection and revolution that have been developed by political scientists.

It seems to me that we must figure out what power
is, and how it is preserved, expended and replenished.
In particular, we need to look at the difficult, but cen-
trally important, question of the willingness of persons
to expend power. This is an area of particular interest
to me, one that I want to develop more thoroughly in a
study I am now planning for the megalopolis of Southern
California. I am not going to concentrate on single communities because it seems to me that the usefulness of
single community studies is declining rapidly in a pluralistic decision structure.

THE COMMUNITY AS SUBSYSTEM

Given the current vogue in political science for
systems theory, I think the community would certainly
lend itself to some future studies as a subsystem. The
systems studies, of course, concentrate on outputs or
lack of outputs. It seems to me somebody might well
spend some time relating this back to community power
theory. That is to say, surely outputs or failures at
outputs must tell us something about the efficacy of the
use of power. The theorists in systems work generally
ignore, of course, the little black box, and I'm suggesting that maybe we should try to figure out the relationships between the community subsystem and the use of
power. Or if we don't want to do that, at least we could
somehow compare the inputs in terms of power with the
outputs in terms of policies.

THE COMMUNITY AS ECOLOGY OF IDEOLOGIES

I would also suggest that another vogue in political
science lends itself to community power studies, and this
is viewing the community as an ecology of ideologies. We

haven't done a great deal on this. Williams and I did some work on images of the ideal community as a basis for policy decisions, but it seems to me that we made the connecting links between the ideologies of leaders and followers badly, if at all. We need a better analysis. We can view what was once considered in the Lynd sense as "the community power structure" as an ideology or set of ideologies relative to the good community and the good life. We can compare leaders' ideologies with those of persons in the working class and subworking class, members of society who are increasingly organized today and therefore presumably possessors of increasing power.

We also have the New Left with its concentration on the problems of the ghetto. To some extent the efforts of the New Left represent an attempt to idealize once again the unknown individual, the powerless individual, and to try to give him power. The New Left has a strong potential source of power in the ghetto. And the Far Right, of course, continues what I call a "politics of nostalgia and paranoia," in contrast to the "politics of conscience," which characterizes the New Left and the "politics of frustration" of the Black Power movement. All of these political movements operate within the same area, all deal with the same governmental structure, and all are essentially ideological positions seeking to influence public policy.

COALITION BUILDING

Then getting back to what I said about looking at the question of willingness to expend resources, I have an interest in the question of coalition building. If the community is an ecology of ideologies, or an ecology of power sets, then maybe we should concentrate on how to build what Riker would call a "minimal winning coalition" within a community.

There are indications in political science that unless the concept of power is better qualified, and

soon, and unless systems theorists are able to explain
how inputs are converted into outputs, efforts at theory
development are likely to concentrate upon decisions.
This approach offers political scientists (and perhaps
sociologists) an opportunity to make analytical progress
through borrowing from sophisticated economic theories.
The decision has been considered the appropriate unit for
political science for more than two decades. It is currently tending to replace the power and group-interest
theories of the 1950's. Its prospects remain obscure,
but they continue to be viewed optimistically by increasing numbers of political scientists. Perhaps our goal
ought to be to reconcile power and decision theories.

Problems exist in relating some of the emerging
theory in decisionmaking and choice making to community
power structure theory. For example, in small communities, the unanimity principle of small group theory probably ought to apply to the use of power or decisionmaking
in the community. In large cities we should have something akin to Riker's "size principle" in operation.
Logically, the ruling group ought to be the smallest
group that can control. But in fact, according to the
kinds of studies done by Edward Banfield and others, the
opposite is the case. Strenuous efforts are made in
large cities to avoid applying the size principle. Thus,
some effort has to be made to try to bring various bits
of emerging theory together so that at least one doesn't
unexplain what the other "explains."

POSSESSION OF INFLUENCE

And finally, perhaps we need to look more carefully
at the question of the possession of influence (more
accurately, the possession of resources) by various
groups in the community and their willingness to commit
those resources at various levels of government. Then we
might try to produce some kind of calculus of the allocation of power or influence in the community. If we could
know more about the elasticity (or rigidity) of demand

for certain types of services--police protection, sufficient water pressure, neighborhood recreation areas,
restaurant inspection and the like--we would know much
more about the kinds of pressures for action that could
be brought upon local officials and community leaders.

It is commonly assumed, for example, that virtually
nothing is being done about smog in Southern California
because the power holders are unwilling to commit the
vast resources that would be required for an effective
attack on the problem. But what is perhaps much more
important is the possibility that they are able to pursue
this policy because the typical citizen is unconcerned
about smog and accepts it as a given, not as a challenge.
Yet, we do not know this to be the case. It is one of
the loose ends we must tie together in developing community power theory.

NOTES

[1] Robert A. Dahl, "The Concept of Power," *Behavioral Science*, 2(3): 201-215 (1957).

[2] William H. Form and Delbert C. Miller, *Industry, Labor, and Community* (New York: Harper & Row, 1960).

[3] Edward C. Banfield, *Big City Politics* (New York: Random House, 1965).

[4] Robert S. and Helen M. Lynd, *Middletown* (New York: Harcourt, Brace & Co., 1929), and *Middletown in Transition* (New York: Harcourt, Brace & Co., 1937).

[5] Oliver P. Williams and Charles R. Adrian, *Four Cities: A Study in Comparative Policy Making* (Philadelphia: University of Pennsylvania Press, 1963).

Dimensions of Power Structure: Some Problems in Conceptualization and Measurement

by CHARLES M. BONJEAN

University of Texas, Austin

CONTENTS

TABLES

21

Although the study of community power has come a long way since Hunter turned on the ignition switch in 1953,[1] the current literature indicates the need to refocus our attention on problems of conceptualization and measurement before we plunge too far ahead with comparative studies. Otherwise, they too may be as unrelated and almost as atheoretical as the flood of case studies that preceded them.

The purpose of this presentation is to outline a power structure typology and to discuss some of the problems it presents. No claim is made that this typology--a modification of one Olson and I set forth in 1964--should be accepted as a model.[2] Rather, the goals are much more modest: to synthesize previous findings, to conceptualize the major differences in power structures described in the literature, and to suggest some problems (and an occasional tentative solution) in regard to their measurement.

A TYPOLOGY OF COMMUNITY POWER STRUCTURE

Because extreme or "ideal type" constructs have been useful in other comparative studies, we take as our point of departure two polar types. The first is based on an exaggeration of Hunter's 1953 findings, and the second on an overstatement of Dahl's 1961 description of New Haven.[3] The former would be *covert elitism* where:

(1) no top decisionmakers occupy positions in the formal structure of government;

(2) none are recognized as key decisionmakers by the community at large;

(3) each exercises influence in all "important" issue areas; and

(4) there is consensus among leaders on ideology and thus on priorities and policy directions.

At the other extreme would be *legitimate pluralism*, best described by the opposites of the previous four statements:

(1) decisionmakers hold formal political office;

(2) they are visible, recognized as key decisionmakers by the community at large;

(3) each is influential only in issue areas related to the formal position he holds; and

(4) constituents are heterogeneous and the leaders represent divergent values, priorities and directions.

In short, four dimensions seem to be required to describe and differentiate the salient aspects of elitist and pluralist structures: legitimacy, visibility, scope of influence and the distribution of values. That these dimensions also differentiate between power structures falling between the two extremes is shown by a number of exercises, including an attempt to differentiate Dahl's five types of power structures.[4] Although space does not permit full discussion of our typology, mention of some of the problems of conceptualization and measurement associated with each dimension may aid future research on power structure.

THE DIMENSION OF LEGITIMACY

While the concept of *legitimacy* may at first appear to have a clear empirical referent (at least we thought it did in 1964), it raises a major problem, that of defining "formal political structure," "public office," or "authority position." We could take a restrictive view and classify as legitimate only those elected or appointed officials associated with formal government: mayor, council members, city manager, local party chairmen, county commissioners. But in most cases this would involve characterizing as "nonlegitimate" an extremely heterogeneous category of leaders ranging from the president of the League of Women Voters to the president of the Chamber of Commerce and the chairman of the board of a local bank. This would depart not only from the political attitudes of our society, but also from the viewpoints of most pluralist scholars. In other words, it is likely that some formal positions outside the structure of city and county government are also, to some degree, legal-rational or legitimate positions in the context of the local political institution.

Greer and Orleans have suggested the concept "para-political" to refer to positions which, although not specifically oriented to politics in their major activities, often become overtly political.[5] Although the concept needs to be sharpened, it would include the president of the Chamber of Commerce and the president of the League of Women Voters, but not the bank board chairman. If parapolitical positions possess some legal-rational authority, but less than that attached to formal political offices, then the legitimacy of leadership positions must be seen as a variable rather than as a dichotomous attribute. The complications this introduces for measurement should be obvious. Still, when rough indices of legitimacy (constructed by assigning different weights to political, parapolitical and nonlegitimate leaders) were used to compare seven power structures in southwestern cities, the differences between cities were so large that problems of precision seemed secondary.

THE DIMENSION OF VISIBILITY

Leader visibility means the degree to which leaders are recognized by those members of the community outside the "inner circle." While it is mentioned or implied in many power structure studies, this concept is seldom given central attention and has only rarely been treated in a systematic manner,[6] possibly because investigators have assumed that visibility and legitimacy overlap.

They would do so if all community leaders held political or parapolitical offices and if community interest in politics were high. The reverse, however, is not equally true. Leaders who do not hold formal positions may or may not be recognized outside the inner circle. As Abu-Laban has suggested, in some cases they may resist visibility: in others, community residents may fail to seek potentially available knowledge.[7] Whatever its source, visibility affects the degree to which anticipated reactions will be considered in decisionmaking and thus the degree to which power relationships in a community approach symmetry.[8]

Visibility may be assessed by the reputational approach, treating the nominees themselves as a panel of judges or informants rather than as leaders. It is assumed that even if these nominees are not leaders, at least their perceptions of the leadership structure are more accurate than those of the original panel selected by the investigator. Nominees' nominations and rankings are then analyzed and compared with the other informants' nominations. Table I shows that the comparisons yield three types of leaders:

(1) *Visible leaders:* those individuals nominated as frequently by the "knowledgeables" as by the other informants.

(2) *Concealed leaders:* those nominated more frequently by the knowledgeables than by the other informants.

(3) *Symbolic leaders:* those nominated more frequently by the other informants than by the knowledgeables.[9]

The differential visibility of leadership structures may be assessed by comparing the proportion of leaders identified as visible. Such a measure has been used in at least 15 communities. As Table II indicates, the proportion of visible leaders has ranged from 27 to 86 percent. Because essentially the same methods were used in

TABLE I

RANKING OF 16 LEADERS BY THEMSELVES AND BY NONLEADERS[a]

Name of leader	Total sample (N=38)	Rank-ing by leaders (N=10)	Ranking by non-leaders (N=28)	Differ-ence	Leader type[b]
Neal Allen	1	1	2	-1	v
James Barton	2	2	3.5	-1.5	v
George Welles	3	10	1	9	s
Mike Reynolds	4	3	5	-2	v
Tom White	5	9	6	3	v
R.V. Daniels	6	4	11	-7	c
Terry Jones	7	13	7	6	s
Percy Roberts	8	17	3.5	13.5	s
Charles Martin	9	11	12	-1	v
Thomas Mintler	10	14	9.5	4.5	s
A.G. Curtis	11	7	13	-6	c
Richard Murphy	12	16	8	8	s
Harold Smith	13	5	14	-9	c
Harold B. Green	14	6	15	-9	c
LeRoy Barton	15	8	16	-8	c
Harvey Harris	16	15	9.5	5.5	s
Dan Morley	...	12	....	-5	c

[a]From Charles M. Bonjean, "Community Leadership: A Case Study and Conceptual Refinement," *American Journal of Sociology*, 68(6) (1963). See p. 675.

[b]Leader type: v, visible; s, symbolic; c, concealed.

TABLE II

LEGITIMACY AND VISIBILITY OF 15 COMMUNITY POWER STRUCTURES

Community	Population (1960)	Percent of leaders visible	Legitimacy score
Charlotte, N.C.[a]	201,600	82.0	.77[b]
Austin, Texas[c]	186,500	28.6	.36[d]
Winston-Salem, N.C.[a]	111,100	80.0	.75[b]
High Point, N.C.[a]	62,000	38.0	.62[b]
Burlington, N.C.[a]	33,200	29.0	.65[b]
Victoria, Texas[c]	33,000	38.9	.63[d]
"Indiana City"[e]	32,000	31.6	f
Carlsbad, N.M.[c]	25,500	27.3	.48[d]
Alice, Texas[c]	20,900	42.9	.38[d]
Edinburg, Texas[c]	18,700	40.0	.48[d]
San Marcos, Texas[c]	12,700	34.3	.47[d]
"Fretolm," Saskatchewan[g]	4,300	61.5	f
"Westnoor," Saskatchewan[g]	2,800	82.0	f

"Hollobreks," Saskatchewan[g]	1,100	66.7	f
"Sondaris," Saskatchewan[g]	600	86.0	f

[a]Charles M. Bonjean and Lewis F. Carter, "Legitimacy and Visibility: Leadership Structures Related to Four Community Systems," *Pacific Sociological Review,* 8(1): 16–20 (1965).

[b]Political and parapolitical leaders assigned the same weight.

[c]Bonjean, study of seven southwestern communities, power structures and leader attitudes; data analysis in process.

[d]Political leaders weighted 1.00; parapolitical, .50.

[e]Delbert C. Miller and James L. Dirkson, "The Identification of Visible, Concealed and Symbolic Leaders in a Small Indiana City: A Replication of the Bonjean-Noland Study of Burlington, North Carolina," *Social Forces,* 43(4): 548–555 (1965).

[f]Not available.

[g]Serena Phillett, "An Analysis of Community Influence: Some Conceptual and Methodological Considerations," unpublished M.A. Thesis, University of Alberta, 1963.

all of these communities, the extreme variation cannot
be written off as a product of different methodologies.[10]

Other studies have shown that differences in the
visibility of leadership structures appear to be related
to community characteristics, and that visible, concealed and symbolic leaders have different personal characteristics.[11]

SCOPE OF INFLUENCE

Our third dimension indicates whether one leader or
set of leaders participates in a wide range of issues,
or whether each issue area is the preserve of a different
set of leaders. It tells us whether scope of influence
is wide or narrow, overlapping or discrete. This question may be investigated by either the decisional or the
modified reputational approach. Dahl's study exemplifies
the former; Table III shows a questionnaire tally
designed for the latter method.

The key problem associated with either orientation
is that of selecting issues or developing criteria for
their selection. Manifest content, cost, participation,
the number of individuals affected by the outcome and
other criteria have been used to select those issues that
investigators term "important."[12] Polling of leaders is
a less common way to assess the importance of issues, yet
this type of reputational selection may be preferable to
the use of "objective" criteria.[13] Where both are used,
the reputational should perhaps be given more weight.

To the degree that communities and their leadership
structures vary, one would expect issue saliency to vary
as well. Yet while many of the criteria could theoretically indicate some variation among the issues that are
salient in different communities, their use would be more
likely to minimize such differences. For example, fluoridation will invariably be a salient issue if "the number
of individuals affected by the outcome" is the criterion
used. Indeed it has been the focus of several

TABLE IV

LEADERS' RANKINGS OF IMPORTANCE OF ISSUE AREAS IN SIX SOUTHWESTERN COMMUNITIES

Issue	Rank in Community				San Marcos	Austin
	Edinburg	Carlsbad	Victoria	Alice		
1. Industrial development	1	1	5	2	1	3
2. Educational facilities	2	5	1	1	2	4
3. Combating crime and delinquency	6	3	2	4	6	1
4. Urban renewal	4	2	4	7	3	7.5
5. Hospitals and medical facilities	3	7	3	3	5	2
6. Poverty programs	5	4	8	5	4	5
7. Tax problems	8	8	6	8	7	6
8. Relations with Mexican-Americans	7	6	7	6	8	9
9. Relations with Negroes	10	9	9	9	9	7.5
10. Fluoridation	9	10	10	10	10	10
Number of informants in each community:	46	62	51	47	45	39

characterized by conceptual ambiguity and few direct
empirical tests. Some of the problems stem from an
assumed relationship between consensus (agreement in matters of opinion) and cohesion (the attraction of a group
for its members). It is sometimes assumed that consensus
will lead to, or is a part of, cohesion. The latter is
then measured sociometrically and used as an indicator of
the former. But the small-group literature in sociology
suggests this may not be the case, that "...neither
variable is necessarily a cause or consequence of the
other."[15]

Both concepts, cohesion and consensus, may be important in the eventual development of a usable power structure typology, but consensus seems to be more relevant to
current elitist and pluralist models. The major problem
in conceptualizing and measuring the consensus-divergence
dimension is that of specification of referents. Do we
measure consensus or divergence with regard to general
orientations such as values and ideologies, or with
regard to more specific sentiments such as opinions or
decisional preferences?

General orientations, values and ideologies can be
and have been studied in the context of consensus/diver-
gence. The outstanding effort to date, in terms both of
conceptualization and measurement, is *The Rulers and the
Ruled*, whose authors, Agger, Goldrich and Swanson are
concerned with the extent to which political leadership
is characterized by single or multiple ideologies. Yet
to use their approach in more than a few communities
would be a task to discourage even the most ambitious.[16]

More specific referents may be better suited to comparative designs involving a fairly large number of
cities. As an example, Scoble's study of Bennington,
Vermont shows how decisional preferences may be used to
assess the consensus/divergence dimension of leadership
structure.[17] Scoble examined leaders' positions on three
different categories of issues, which were then treated
as roll-call data. The data were analyzed by the Rice-
Turner indices of cohesion (actually consensus) and

likeness.[18]   The use of such indices has a number of
advantages:

(1)   the fact that they are true ratio scales make
      them especially adaptable to comparative
      research;

(2)   data collection and analysis are fairly simple
      and straightforward (at least when compared to
      attempts such as those of Agger, et al.); and

(3)   if the investigator has also studied scope of
      influence and has determined which issues are
      "important," he can be relatively certain that
      he is also exploring the important areas of
      consensus and divergence.

The major problem associated with the use of such
indices is the requirement that data be dichotomized.
Thus, unless the issues actually involve choosing one of
two alternatives, the use of the Rice-Turner indices may
oversimplify the nature of divergence or overestimate the
degree of consensus.   This problem was apparently recognized by Scoble, for he also reported both the leaders'
scores on two attitude scales and the distribution of
their attitudes toward state and national candidates and
issues, of which all but one involved more than two
alternatives.[19]

Thus it appears that the use of attitude scales may
be one of the most promising ways to measure consensus/
divergence.   In addition, it provides other relevant
information about the nature of leadership structure.
But although attitude measurement has been one of the
most significant developments in the social sciences in
the last several decades, little use has been made of
such scales in community power research.[20]

Some relatively valid and reliable scales widely
used in other areas of our disciplines--for example, the
California F Scale and McClosky's Conservatism Scale--
approximate the assessment of ideology, or at least some

of its important elements. The F Scale, in addition to
measuring prejudice without appearing to have this aim
and without mentioning the name of any minority group, is
said to yield "...a valid estimate of antidemocratic tendencies at the personality level."[21] Similarly, the
McClosky Scale is based upon "...those attitudes and
values that continually recur among acknowledged conservative thinkers and that appear to comprise the invariant
elements of the conservative outlook."[22]

Either or both of these scales could serve as important instruments for assessing the nature and distribution of values within a leadership structure. This
investigator, however, has been able to find only two
uses of the F Scale and none of the McClosky Scale in
the literature of community power.[23] Indeed, the assessment of leader attitudes, including their degree of consensus or divergence, appears to constitute a major
research gap in this substantive area. It may be that
methodological problems are to blame. Some of the more
important problems are associated with

(1) measures of dispersion--of obvious importance
     for consensus/divergence;

(2) the ordinal nature of the scales;

(3) the lack of correlation between divergence on
     one attitude (such as conservatism) and diver-
     gence on others (such as authoritarianism); and

(4) the development and use of criteria for select-
     ing the attitude scales to be used.

CONCLUSION

The four dimensions of legitimacy, visibility, scope
of influence and distribution of influence enable us to
conceptualize and differentiate the structural arrangements found in the community power literature. They

raise a number of questions about the nature of power at
the community level. And their use, or the use of similar typologies, may provide a theoretical basis for
making comparative community power studies truly comparative.

NOTES

Author's comment: This paper is revised and expanded from a portion of an earlier article. See Charles M. Bonjean and David M. Olson, "Community Leadership: Directions of Research," *Administrative Science Quarterly*, 9(3): 278-300 (1964). See especially pp. 289-295.

[1] Floyd Hunter, *Community Power Structure* (Chapel Hill: The University of North Carolina Press, 1953).

[2] Charles M. Bonjean and David M. Olson, "Community Leadership: Directions of Research," *Administrative Science Quarterly*, 9(3): 278-300 (1964).

[3] Robert A. Dahl, *Who Governs? Democracy and Power in an American City* (New Haven: Yale University Press, 1961).

[4] Ibid., pp. 184-189. See, for example, the following list:

TYPES OF COMMUNITY INFLUENCE STRUCTURES

I   Covert Elite
   A. Members do not hold political office
   B. Constituents unaware of leaders and their decisions
   C. Broad scope of influence
   D. Consensus on values

II Independent Sovereignties
   A. Members do not hold political office
   B. Constituents unaware of leaders and their decisions
   C. Scopes narrow and not overlapping
   D. Consensus within each grouping

III   Rival Sovereignties
    A.   Members do not hold political office
    B.   Constituents aware of at least some leaders and most issues
    C.   Scopes narrow and overlapping
    D.   Consensus within each grouping, divergence between them

IV   Interest Groups and a Coalition of Coalitions
    A.   Some members hold political office, some do not
    B.   Constituents aware of some leaders and most issues
    C.   Scope narrow within each group
    D.   Consensus within groups, some consensus between them

V   Competing Political Parties and Consent
    A.   Members hold political office
    B.   Constituents aware of leaders and their decisions
    C.   Scope related to official area
    D.   Divergent values

[5] Scott Greer and Peter Orleans, "The Mass Society and the Parapolitical Structure," *American Sociological Review*, 27(5): 634-646 (1962).

[6] A few significant exceptions include Baha Abu-Laban, "Leader Visibility in a Local Community," *Pacific Sociological Review*, 4(2): 73-78 (1961); Charles M. Bonjean, "Class, Status and Power Reputation," *Sociology and Social Research*, 49(1): 69-75 (1964); Charles M. Bonjean and Lewis F. Carter, "Legitimacy and Visibility: Leadership Structures Related to Four Community Systems," *Pacific Sociological Review*, 8(1): 16-20 (1965); Delbert C. Miller and James L. Dirkson, "The Identification of Visible, Concealed and Symbolic Leaders in a Small Indiana City: A Replication of the Bonjean-Noland Study of Burlington, North Carolina" *Social Forces*, 43(4): 548-555 (1965); Robert Mills French and Michael Aiken, "Community Power in Cornucopia: A Replication in a Small Community of the Bonjean Technique of Identifying Community Leaders," *Sociological Quarterly*, 9(2): 261-270

(1968); and James D. Preston, "The Search for Community Leaders: A Re-examination of the Reputational Technique," *Sociological Inquiry*, 39(1): 39-47 (1969).

[7] Baha Abu-Laban, "The Reputational Approach in the Study of Community Power: A Critical Evaluation," *Pacific Sociological Review*, 8(1): 35-42 (1965).

[8] See Terry N. Clark, "The Concept of Power: Some Overemphasized and Under-recognized Dimensions--An Examination with Special Reference to the Local Community," *Southwestern Social Science Quarterly*, 48(3): 271-286 (1967), for a discussion of anticipated reactions and reciprocity in power relationships.

[9] A detailed discussion of the techniques used to determine the three types of leaders may be found in Charles M. Bonjean, "Community Leadership: A Case Study and Conceptual Refinement," *American Journal of Sociology*, 68(6): 672-681 (1963), especially 678-679; and in Miller and Dirkson, note 6 above, p. 550.

[10] If the decisional approach in its pure form had been used in some communities and the reputational in others, we might expect such differences. That findings may be an artifact of methods has been suggested by many scholars, including John Walton, "Substance and Artifact: The Current Status of Research on Community Power Structure," *American Journal of Sociology*, 71(4): 430-438 (1966); and Walton, "Discipline, Method, and Community Power: A Note on the Sociology of Knowledge," *American Sociological Review*, 31(5): 684-689 (1966).

[11] Bonjean and Carter, note 6 above, discuss visibility. On personal characteristics, see Bonjean, "Class, Status, and Power Reputation," and Miller and Dirkson, note 6 above. Related findings have been reported by A. Alexander Fanelli, "A Typology of Community Leadership Based on Influence and Interaction within the Leader Subsystem," *Social Forces*, 34(4) 332-338 (1956).

[12] Manifest content categories have been used by Aaron Wildavsky, *Leadership in a Small Town* (Totowa, N.J.: Bedminster Press, 1964), pp. 253-254; M. Kent Jennings,

Community Influentials: The Elites of Atlanta (New York: Free Press of Glencoe, 1964); and Robert E. Agger, Daniel Goldrich and Bert E. Swanson, *The Rulers and the Ruled: Political Power and Impotence in American Communities* (New York: John Wiley and Sons, 1964). Dahl, *Who Governs?* uses cost and participation, while the number of individuals affected by the outcome is used by Nelson Polsby, *Community Power and Political Theory* (New Haven: Yale University Press, 1963), p. 98.

[13] One instance of this approach may be found in Agger, Goldrich and Swanson, note 12 above, pp. 707-710.

[14] The rankings presented in Table IV have considerable face validity. Industrial development probably ranks low in Victoria because the community has been successful in attracting new industry in recent years. On the other hand, Carlsbad's economy has been based primarily on mineral resources that are nearly depleted. It is under-standable that informants there regard industrial devel-opment as their most important problem. In the largest city, Austin, combating crime and delinquency was regard-ed as the most serious problem, while this concern ranked considerably lower in small communities such as San Marcos and Edinburg. While ranking relatively low in each community, the problem of relations with Negroes was perceived as being relatively more important in the city with the largest proportion of Negroes (Austin) and least important in the community with the smallest proportion of Negroes (Edinburg).

[15] J. Rex Enoch and S. Dale McLemore, "On the Meaning of Group Cohesion," *Southwestern Social Science Quarterly*, 48(2): 174-180 (1967). See especially p. 178.

[16] For a description of their techniques see Agger, Goldrich and Swanson, note 12 above, pp. 1-32, 720-730.

[17] Harry Scoble, "Leadership Hierarchies and Political Issues in a New England Town," pp. 117-145 in Morris Janowitz, ed., *Community Political Systems* (New York: The Free Press of Glencoe, 1961). See especially pp. 120-123.

[18] Ibid., p. 124 and p. 143.

42

[19] Scoble, loc. cit.

[20] Such scales have been administered to formal political officials, but seldom to the other types of leaders identified in power structure research. Among the exceptions are Scoble, loc. cit., and Yasumasa Kuroda, "Psychological Aspects of Community Power Structure: Leaders and Rank-and-File Citizens in Reed Town, Japan," *Southwestern Social Science Quarterly*, 48(3): 433-442 (1967), and Robert Presthus, *Men at the Top: A Study in Community Power* (New York: Oxford University Press, 1964). See especially Presthus, pp. 321-367.

[21] T.W. Adorno, et al., *The Authoritarian Personality* (New York: Harper and Brothers, 1950), pp. 222-223.

[22] Herbert McClosky, "Conservatism and Personality," *American Political Science Review*, 52(1): 27-45 (1958). See especially p. 30.

[23] Kuroda, loc. cit. and Presthus, op. cit.

Community Structure, Decisionmaking, Budget Expenditures and Urban Renewal in 51 American Communities

by TERRY N. CLARK
University of Chicago

CONTENTS

TABLES

FIGURES

During much of the 1950's and early 1960's, studies of community decisionmaking were largely concerned with conceptualizing and measuring the leadership and influence patterns within local communities. The central focus of the research tended to be some variation of Dahl's question, "Who Governs?", and nearly all empirical investigations took the form of case studies of individual communities.

However, by the end of the 1950's, a number of researchers had begun comparative studies of two or more communities. There were several reasons for this new trend: discontent with the limited generalizations that could be derived from individual case studies; belief that the methodological difficulties of measuring "power structures" could be at least partially resolved by comparative research; and--not a negligible factor--increased research funds. Initially, the questions posed were essentially the same as those in the earlier case studies. Systematic differences nevertheless began to emerge in the decision-making patterns of various communities, and a broader range of questions gradually came to be perceived as essential for understanding community decision-making processes.

To determine Who Governs, it became necessary also to ascertain Where, When, and With What Effects.[1] This series of questions focused attention on those structural characteristics of a community that predispose it toward one or another pattern of decisionmaking. The new questions also disposed of an apt criticism of the earlier studies, that they failed to portray the impact of one or another pattern of decisionmaking on concrete community outputs. That is, a community's influence structure is best understood by examining what caused it to develop as well as the consequences of its activity.

47

METHODS OF COMPARATIVE STUDY

With the guiding questions reformulated in this fashion, researchers began to elaborate a series of comparative propositions that would specify answers under varying conditions.[2] And although it has been easier to elaborate propositions than to test them, several procedures for testing propositions have recently been devised.

A first, admittedly crude, method is to compare two or three individual community case studies conducted by different persons, focusing on the concomitant variations in community structures, decision-making patterns, and outputs.[3] Although better than generalizing from a single case, this procedure has definite limitations. There is the difficulty of determining whether varying research methods can yield comparable results, as well as the simple lack of information on theoretically important variables. These constitute formidable obstacles.

A second, improved variation is the comparison of results from two, three or four communities investigated by the same researcher or team of researchers, using directly comparable methods and collecting identical data.[4] While this procedure alone has been more successful than the first, the use of both methods has produced significant advances. But while contrasting results from a small number of communities may provide excellent stimulation for generating propositions, as well as illustrative support for them, such limited numbers of cases make it virtually impossible to sort out the complex interplay of variables.

A third type of procedure is the quantitative comparison of relatively large numbers of case studies where problems of comparability loom large.[5] To compound the difficulty, missing information inevitably lowers the n of any given correlation. But despite its drawbacks, this procedure permits more systematic comparisons than do the first two.

A fourth procedure, and the one most satisfactory for testing comparative propositions, is the quantitative study of large numbers of communities, with the collection of identical data in each case, and the use of directly comparable research methods. While the value of this procedure has been recognized for some time, only recently has it been possible to mobilize the necessary human and financial resources for its application.

THE STUDY OF 51 COMMUNITIES

This paper reports on such an undertaking, one in which 51 American communities were investigated by the field staff of the National Opinion Research Center at the University of Chicago, in the largest study of its kind to date. The background history of the study has been reported elsewhere and will not be discussed here except to note that it was a joint undertaking of the International Studies of Values in Politics and the NORC Permanent Community Sample, financed by the National Science Foundation and the McNeil Foundation of Philadelphia.[6]

Characteristics of the 51 Communities

The 51 communities were sampled on the basis of region and population size. Table I presents some of their basic characteristics. Representing 22 different states, cities in the population range of 50,000-750,000 were selected in order to eliminate the somewhat unique metropolises and the smaller communities for which basic census-type statistics were not readily available. As Table I shows, they varied also in selected measures of socioeconomic levels, governmental policy and organizational life.

These rankings represent only a few of the approximately 300 variables for each community, developed through the sources indicated in Table I. The sources themselves were not uniformly conventional or well known.

For example, when we wished to investigate the possible importance of the religious affiliation of the population, we procured religious data from the reports of the National Council of the Churches of Christ. These data are subject to certain imprecisions: they were only estimates, in some cases; in general, they were compiled in 1952; and they were reported by county rather than by city. Because the figures on religious affiliation were obviously crude, and varied so much from one place to another, we initially had strong doubts about using them at all, but decided to include them on a provisional basis.

Then, because of the extensive discussions about the role of voluntary organizations in community life, dating from de Tocqueville to the present, we sought all possible sources of figures concerning membership in organizations that might conceivably influence community decision-making patterns. In certain cities, such as Dallas and Pittsburgh, there is a single organization that reputedly brings together many leading citizens and plays a leading role in public affairs. In a case study of these communities, information on such an organization is, of course, vital.

But since such groups are not found everywhere, and since their composition and functions vary considerably from one community to the next, information is extremely difficult to interpret meaningfully. The ideal solution would be to collect membership figures for an organization that is found in virtually all communities and undertakes generally comparable activities everywhere. The Parent-Teachers Association was one candidate, but as local organizations, PTA's are developed around individual school districts. There is no national PTA organization able to supply membership figures. We considered several other voluntary organizations, but either they were not comparable across communities or membership figures for our sample were impossible to obtain.

The League of Women Voters, however, was ideal from several standpoints. It is perhaps the single most

TABLE I

SELECTED CHARACTERISTICS OF THE 51 COMMUNITIES

Characteristics	Mean	N	Minimum value	Maximum value
Total population[a]	250,786.00	51	50,498.00	750,026.00
Median income[a]	6,186.04	51	4,232.00	9,132.00
Median school years completed[a]	11.05	51	8.80	13.30
Percent foreign born[a]	7.82	51	1.00	19.00
Percent nonwhite[a]	11.82	51	0.00	41.00
Percent income under $3,000[a]	15.86	51	4.00	33.00
Percent unemployed[a]	5.04	51	2.00	8.00
Percent Jewish[b]	2.44	49	0.04	17.69
Percent Catholic[b]	18.57	51	1.02	56.91
Percent Protestant[b]	23.67	51	7.60	65.30
League of Women Voters membership[c]	268.33	49	0.00	995.00
General budget expenditures, 1957[d]	33,633.039	51	1,537.00	217,110.00
Urban renewal expenditures[e]	39,148.636	51	0.00	167,627.00

[a] U.S. Bureau of the Census, *County and City Data Book* (Washington, D.C.: 1966). Data represent central and independent cities in 1960.

[b] *Churches and Church Membership in the United States* (New York: National Council of the Churches of Christ in the USA, 1956). Figures indicate membership in religious institutions. In some cases they are only estimates.

[c] Supplied by the Washington headquarters of the League of Women Voters of the United States. Data are for cities, as of January 1, 1967. Thanks are due to Mrs. Paul Cleveland for making these data available.

[d] U.S. Bureau of the Census, *Compendium of City Government Finances* (Washington, D.C.: 1960).

[e] U.S. Urban Renewal Administration, *Urban Renewal Project Characteristics* (Washington, D.C.: 1965).

important civic voluntary organization in American communities, and frequently becomes involved in significant
local issues. While not identical in every locality, the
activities of the League from one community to the next
are carefully observed by the national organization: the
local League in at least one of our communities had been
disbanded after involvement in activities beyond those
sanctioned by the organization's bylaws. The national
headquarters also maintains accurate membership figures
on the local organizations and generously made them
available to us for analysis.

Data Collection Procedures

In addition to these data from central sources,
other material was drawn from a series of interviews on
matters such as political organization and decisionmaking. In earlier studies, and on the basis of preliminary
fieldwork in several communities, we had found about a
dozen persons from different sectors particularly well
informed about local affairs. These were not necessarily
the most active participants, but were generally knowledgeable informants. To collect as much information as
possible, so as to maximize reliability and validity
while minimizing costs, we decided to interview 11 stra-
tegically placed informants in each community. These
were: the mayor, the chairmen of the Democratic and
Republican parties, the president of the largest bank,
the editor of the newspaper with the largest circulation,
the president of the Chamber of Commerce, the president
of the bar association, the head of the largest labor
union, the health commissioner, the urban renewal director and the director of the last major hospital fund
drive.[7]

Interview schedules concentrated on the informants'
particular institutional realms, but most also contained
a core set of items dealing with general community
issues. The professional field staff of NORC conducted
the interviews in January 1967, generally with one inter-
viewer in each community. To maximize reliability,
interviewers received a general report about the study as

well as detailed interview instructions, including a list of substitutes for unavailable interviewees.

Issue Areas

To maintain comparability, informants in each community were interviewed about the same four issues: urban renewal, the election of the mayor, air pollution and the antipoverty program. These four were selected because they tended to involve different types of community actors in differing relationships with one another.[8] A mayoral election, for example, tends to mobilize the various community sectors along traditional lines of political cleavage as detailed by studies of voting behavior: income, education, religion, and the like. Urban renewal, on the other hand, may divide a community along traditional political lines. But, due to the importance of outside funds, it may also become a general distributive issue wherein virtually all members of the community benefit from funds supplied largely by the federal government.

The antipoverty issue is similar to urban renewal in that it relies on outside funds and requires no reallocation of community resources. But unlike urban renewal, which may be turned toward diverse subsectors of the community depending on the content of the program, the antipoverty program is of course largely oriented toward assisting the poorer sectors of the community. (There may, of course, be substantial indirect benefits to other sectors.)

Air pollution, in contrast, requires direct and often expensive sacrifices by the industrial sector of the community for the benefit of the community as a whole. Thus two issues--mayoral elections and air pollution--tend to involve the redistribution of local resources, although the directions and amounts of reallocation are subject to varying definitions. The two other issues--urban renewal and poverty--principally involve distribution within the community of resources supplied from outside. They also imply close relationships with higher level governmental officials outside the community.

All four issue areas need the support of local government to implement basic decisions. And, of course, insofar as any decision-making structure exists within a community, it will channel and redirect the activities within these various areas.[9] But it is just this decision-making structure that is illuminated by comparison of the patterns of influence in the four different issue areas.

The Ersatz Decisional Method

We attempted to measure the community decision-making structure by using what we termed "the ersatz decisional method." We examined the number of major actors involved in each issue area, and the degree to which decisionmakers overlapped from one issue area to the next. For each issue area, we posed a series of questions that focused on these points:

(1) Who initiated action on the issue?

(2) Who supported this action?

(3) Who opposed this action?[10]

(4) What was the nature of the bargaining process? Who negotiated with whom?

(5) What was the outcome? Whose views tended to prevail?

The cross classification of the five decisional stages with the four issue areas generated for each community a 20-cell matrix, which furnished the basis for our index of centralization.

Most theoretical discussions of centralization of authority, pluralism (here understood as decentralization), and related concepts have isolated the two basic dimensions included in our index. The first is *participation*: the larger the number of actors involved in

community decisionmaking, the greater the decentralization. Second is *overlap*: the less similar the cluster
of actors in one issue area are to those in adjoining
issue areas, the greater the decentralization.[11]

To combine these conceptual dimensions in a single
index, we counted the number of actors named by our
informants, but we counted each actor only once even if
he was named in more than one issue area. Then, because
a particular issue area did not exist in a few communities (see Table II), after we had obtained the number of
actors by summing as described above, we divided by the
number of issue areas present in the community.

TABLE II

COMMUNITIES IN WHICH
ISSUE AREAS WERE ABSENT

Issue Area	Number of Communities
Air pollution	5
Urban renewal	2
Poverty program	1

A few examples may clarify this procedure.

Consider first a situation regarded as that of a
highly centralized or monolithic community: the mayor
initiated action on a decision, was supported by the
downtown businessmen and opposed by the labor unions and
the newspaper. The mayor was the major entrepreneur in
bargaining among the various groups, and the mayor-
businessmen coalition prevailed. Under such circumstances, the total number of actors in the issue would be
four: mayor, businessmen, labor unions and newspaper.
If these same four actors, again playing the same roles,
were the only ones involved in three other issues, there
would still only be a total of four actors in all issue
areas. Dividing the number of actors by the number of
issue areas, would yield a final score for the community
of one. This centralized community would thus rank near
the bottom of our scale of decentralization.

On the other hand, if we consider a situation generally regarded as more decentralized, where, for example,
five different actors were involved in each of four issue
areas, the total number of actors would be 20, and,
dividing by the number of issue areas, the community
score would come to five. Applying this same procedure,
we computed a decentralization score for each of the 51
communities. These scores are presented in Table III.

There were a number of ambiguities and problems in
dealing with the centralization of decisionmaking. One
was the problem of identifying distinct actors. For
example, in one community three labor leaders might be
named as actors, while in another only "the labor unions"
would be specified. We reasoned that different individuals closely similar in status should not be counted the
same as three individuals from three differing sectors of
the community. Therefore we devised a code of some 73
community statuses and considered that a separate actor
would be counted for each status named. But two persons
occupying the same status were counted only once. A
single individual could thus be counted as two actors if
he were named in two different issue areas as the occu-
pant of two distinct statuses, e.g., county judge and
chairman of a neighborhood organization. Some might dis-
agree with this interpretation, but we reasoned that it
was more logical to weight by the involvement of community institutions, rather than by the involvement of
individuals.

Another ambiguity arose from conflicting or missing
information from different informants. Our solution was
to count each new status mentioned by any informant as
nominating a new actor. But if a status were mentioned
several times by different informants, it was counted
only once. There were, however, slight but systematic
differences in the number of actors named by different
informants. For this reason, we constructed weights for
the different informants, based on the mean number of
actors they named who were not mentioned by any other
informant. The weights were constructed for informants
in the 36 communities where no informants were missing.
(See Table IV) Then, in the 15 communities where one or

TABLE III

INDEX SCORES OF DECENTRALIZED DECISION-MAKING STRUCTURES FOR THE 51 COMMUNITIES

0. Akron, Ohio	7.50	26. Milwaukee, Wis.	7.75
1. Albany, N.Y.	6.63	27. Minneapolis, Minn.	8.00
2. Amarillo, Texas	3.33	28. Newark, N.J.	9.13
3. Atlanta, Ga.	6.50	29. Palo Alto, Calif.	6.50
4. Berkeley, Calif.	5.92	30. Pasadena, Calif.	5.50
5. Birmingham, Ala.	5.88	31. Phoenix, Ariz.	7.75
6. Bloomington, Minn.	4.45	32. Pittsburgh, Penn.	7.75
7. Boston, Mass.	7.25	33. St. Louis, Mo.	8.00
8. Buffalo, N.Y.	8.67	34. St. Paul, Minn.	8.50
9. Cambridge, Mass.	8.67	35. St. Petersburg, Fla.	6.75
10. Charlotte, N.C.	6.25	36. Salt Lake City, Utah	7.13
11. Clifton, N.J.	5.90	37. San Francisco, Calif.	7.75
12. Duluth, Minn.	5.25	38. Santa Ana, Calif.	6.50
13. Euclid, Ohio	6.93	39. San Jose, Calif.	5.63
14. Fort Worth, Texas	6.75	40. Santa Monica, Calif.	6.33
15. Fullerton, Calif.	6.45	41. Schenectady, N.Y.	5.75
16. Gary, Ind.	6.75	42. Seattle, Wash.	7.50
17. Hamilton, Ohio	6.00	43. South Bend, Ind.	7.00
18. Hammond, Ind.	7.75	44. Tampa, Fla.	8.25
19. Indianapolis, Ind.	9.00	45. Tyler, Texas	7.67
20. Irvington, N.J.	7.67	46. Utica, N.Y.	9.38
21. Jacksonville, Fla.	6.25	47. Waco, Texas	3.25
22. Long Beach, Calif.	4.75	48. Warren, Mich.	5.50
23. Malden, Mass.	8.50	49. Waterbury, Conn.	8.75
24. Manchester, N.H.	4.97	50. Waukegan, Ill.	7.67
25. Memphis, Tenn.	6.38		

Mean Score for the 51 Communities = 6.792

more informants were unavailable for an interview, the
centralization index score for that community was
increased by the amount of the weight for the missing
informant(s).

Still other questions arose from what might be
termed the dynamics of the decision-making process:
within a given issue area, how should one perceive the
relationships between the various stages of a decision?
Is initiating action more important than supporting it?
Does a heavy involvement of actors at the opposition
stage imply greater conflict and a more decentralized
decision-making process? If the answers to these two
questions were clear affirmatives, they would imply,
methodologically, a disproportionate weighting of the
actors involved at the initiation and opposition stages.
But given the absence in this area of any theory sufficiently rigorous to permit the researcher to assign specific weights, we made the conservative choice of assigning equal value to each actor in the issue area, regardless of the stage at which he became involved.[12]

COMMUNITY STRUCTURE, DECISIONMAKING AND OUTPUTS

An earlier article formulated a series of 34 propositions relating community structural characteristics
(including the demographic, economic, legal-political,
cultural) to centralized and decentralized patterns of
decisionmaking.[13] Subsequently refining certain of these
propositions, we added several others relating decision-
making patterns to outputs, and subsumed a number of the
discrete propositions under a more general formulation:

*The greater the horizontal and vertical differentia-
tion in a social system and the greater the differentiation between potential elites, the more decentralized the
decision-making structure. Without the establishment of
integrative mechanisms, this condition leads to less
coordination between sectors and a lower level of outputs.*[14]

TABLE IV

INFORMANTS AND THE NAMING OF COMMUNITY ACTORS

Informant	Mean no. named as actors	No. of communities with informant unavailable
Chamber of Commerce president	2.08	0
Labor council president	2.14	3
Newspaper editor	1.81	1
Bar Association president	2.69	6
Democratic Party chairman	1.50	2
Republican Party chairman	1.53	1
Mayor	1.53	6

The empirical analysis reported here was primarily oriented toward testing the earlier propositions and the general formulation. We therefore focused on variables for which some theoretical proposition had already been developed, although we were prepared to include others that might account for significant differences in any of the dependent variables.

The Specification of Variables

We inspected a large zero order correlation matrix and isolated variables about which we had specific hypotheses or which correlated highly with the measure of centralization of decisionmaking. Because there was a high intercorrelation of many variables, we performed a series of factor analyses to isolate clusters of variables; then from each cluster, we selected one or two with high factor loadings. Performance of regression analyses reduced the number of independent variables still further. We ended with eight, which together generated multiple correlation coefficients of .475 to .840 with centralization of decisionmaking and the two policy output variables. Before proceeding, let us briefly review each of the variables and output measures utilized.[15]

X_1 = *Population size*.

X_2 = *Community poverty*: percent of population with incomes under \$3,000, percent with fewer than five years of education, percent unemployed, and percent nonwhite. Since all four measures were highly intercorrelated, we simplified the analysis by using percent with income under \$3,000 as an indicator for this cluster.

X_3 = *Industrial activity*: percent of manufacturing establishments in the community with more than 20 employees.

X_4 = *Economic diversification*: classification of communities ranked by Nelson as diversified or financial as distinct from all other communities.[16]

X_5 = *Highly educated population*: median years of schooling completed by the community residents.

X_6 = *Catholic population*: number of members of the Roman Catholic Church in the county, standardized by county population size.

V = *Civic voluntary organization activity*: number of community members in the League of Women Voters, standardized by community population size.

W = *Index of governmental reformism*: constructed from the three governmental characteristics traditionally associated in the United States with "reform" government: professional city manager, nonpartisan elections, and at-large electoral constituencies.[17] Communities with varying combinations of these characteristics were scored as follows:[18]

  3 = manager government, nonpartisan elections, at-large electoral constituencies

  2 = any two of these characteristics

  1 = any one of these characteristics

  0 = none of these characteristics

Y = *Decentralized decision-making structure*: the number and overlap of decisionmakers.

Z_1 = *General budget expenditures*: total budget expenditures of the local community government, standardized by population size.

Z_2 = *Urban renewal expenditures*: total expenditures from federal and local sources on urban renewal projects in the community, up to 1965, standardized by population size.

Table V presents the zero order correlation matrix for these 12 variables.

To test our propositions and evaluate the relative importance of each variable in the model, we computed the relationships among all variables, utilizing a graphic variation of multiple regression analysis: path analysis.[19] (Figures I-V) The reader is referred to the works cited for a more general consideration of the method. We note here only that path analysis is a procedure for representing a causal model of the relationships among a number of different variables. Arrows pointing in the direction of assumed causation connect the variables to one another. Straight arrows represent lines of causation, while double-headed bowed arrows indicate simple intercorrelations not implying dependency relationships. The numerical figure above each arrow leading away from a variable represents the separate contribution made by that variable in each of the directions indicated. Path coefficients may vary from +1 to -1, a negative sign indicating a negative contribution. In addition to these arrows connecting interrelated variables, there is an arrow for a residual error term for each variable dependent on others in the model. Residual error terms may vary from 1 to 0. The larger the error term, the smaller the amount of variance in the dependent variable that is explained by the model.[20]

Although over a long enough period none of the variables is without some influence on the others, at any given time we can without undue difficulty order most of the variables in a causal sequence.[21] Six variables relate to the demographic composition and economic base of the community and, for the present analysis, may be conceived as generally constant: (a) population size,

TABLE V

ZERO ORDER CORRELATION MATRIX OF 11 VARIABLES OF THE MODEL

Variables	X_1	X_2	X_3	X_4	X_5	X_6	V	W	Y	Z_1	Z_2
X_1 Population size											
X_2 Community poverty	.276										
X_3 Industrial activity	-.104	-.141									
X_4 Economic diversification	.516	.334	-.154								
X_5 Highly educated population	-.238	-.339	-.339	.027							
X_6 Catholic population	.037	-.441	.204	-.236	-.322						
V Civic voluntary organizations	-.427	-.269	.049	-.335	.490	.083					
W Reformist government	-.199	.077	-.332	.143	.625	-.425	.276				
Y Decentralized decision-making structure	.384	-.031	-.008	.347	-.332	.254	-.275	-.548			
Z_1 General budget expenditures	.310	-.100	-.062	-.045	-.057	.610	.042	-.015	.237		
Z_2 Urban renewal expenditures	.392	.136	.119	.050	-.297	.454	-.051	-.308	.350	.464	

(b) community poverty, (c) industrial activity, (d) economic diversification, (e) educational level of the population, and (f) percent of the population that is Catholic. We shall examine in turn the impact of each of these
independent variables on five dependent variables:
(1) the level of civic voluntary organization activity,
(2) the form of government, (3) patterns of community
decisionmaking, (4) general budget expenditures, and
(5) urban renewal expenditures.

Civic Voluntary Organization Activity

As one would fully expect from the literature on
voluntary organizations, the educational level of the
population strongly influences the level of civic voluntary organization activity.[22] The second most influential variable was not so predictable: the size of the
Catholic population. While the percent of the community
residents who were Roman Catholics shows no zero order
correlation with voluntary organization activity, the
influence becomes quite sizeable when other variables in
the model are controlled. The impact of the extent of
poverty changed even more radically from the zero order
relation: from a -.269 correlation (Table VI) to a
+.311 path coefficient (Figure I). We might interpret
this finding as suggesting that potential members of the
League of Women Voters generally do not reside in areas
with extensive poverty, but when there is poverty in
their communities, they tend to become active in civic
affairs.

Reform Government

Our findings about the socioeconomic correlates of
reform government characteristics are generally similar
to those reported by earlier students of the subject.[23]
The most influential variable by far is the educational
level of the population: more highly educated populations tend to have reform governments. As Wolfinger and

TABLE VI

CORRELATIONS AND PATH COEFFICIENTS FOR CIVIC VOLUNTARY ORGANIZATION ACTIVITY

Dependent Variable: Civic Voluntary Organization Activity: V

Independent variable	Zero order correlation	Path coefficient
Highly educated population: X_5	.490	.744
Catholic population: X_6	.083	.369
Community poverty: X_2	-.269	.311
Economic diversification: X_4	-.335	-.232
Industrial activity: X_3	.049	.213
Population size: X_1	-.427	-.208

$R = .699$ Variance explained = 43%[a]

$$V^{[b]} = -1031.8581 - \underset{(0.000079)}{0.000122}\ X_1 + \underset{(2.9738)}{5.8659}\ X_2 + \underset{(2.0055)}{3.5166}\ X_3$$

$$- \underset{(33.8527)}{58.3283}\ X_4 + \underset{(17.6693)}{85.2983}\ X_5 + \underset{(1.2286)}{3.0859}\ X_6$$

[a] In the subsequent tables, Variance explained refers to the R^2 corrected for the number of independent variables, not the simple R^2.

[b] Regression coefficients unstandardized; standard errors in parentheses.

FIGURE I

PATH COEFFICIENTS FOR CIVIC
VOLUNTARY ORGANIZATION ACTIVITY

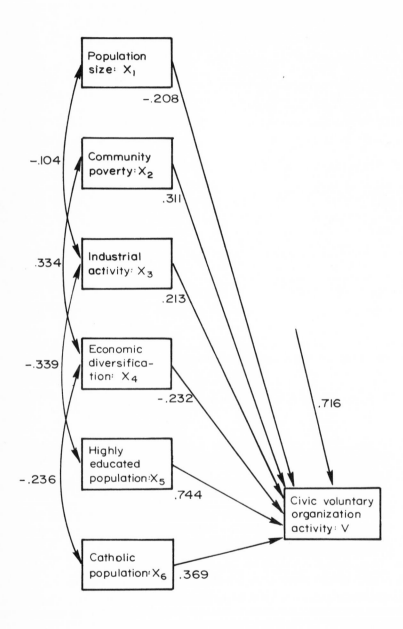

TABLE VII

CORRELATIONS AND PATH COEFFICIENTS FOR INDEX OF REFORM GOVERNMENT

Dependent Variable: Index of Reform Government: W

Independent variable	Zero order correlation	Path coefficient
Highly educated population: X_5	.625	.617
Community poverty: X_2	.077	.265
Population size: X_1	-.199	-.182
Economic diversification: X_4	.143	.110
Industrial activity: X_3	-.332	-.075
Catholic population: X_6	-.425	-.062
Civic voluntary organization activity: V	.276	.012

R = .716   Variance explained = 40%

$$W^a = -5.744202 - \underset{(.000001)}{.000001} X_1 + \underset{(.0122)}{.0469} X_2 - \underset{(.0192)}{.0116} X_3$$
$$+ \underset{(.3243)}{.2592} X_4 + \underset{(.2026)}{.6645} X_5 + \underset{(.0014)}{.0001} V$$

[a] Regression coefficients unstandardized; standard errors in parentheses.

FIGURE II

PATH COEFFICIENTS FOR REFORM GOVERNMENT

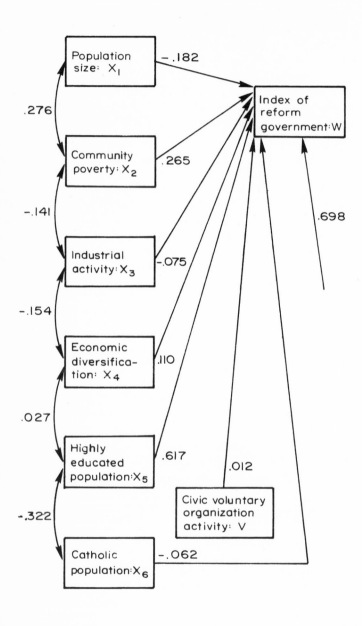

Field point out, this is most characteristic of western communities: our index correlated .645 with a dummy variable representing communities in the western states.

We should call attention, however, to the relationships between reformism and two variables not utilized by earlier authors. The correlation (zero order) with reformism of percent Catholic is -.425, and that of civic activity is .276. Both of these relationships would seem to offer support for the traditional "public regarding-ness" thesis. However, when the other variables (other than region) in the model are introduced, the relationships between these two variables and reformism virtually disappear. (See Table VII and Figure II)

This should presumably be interpreted as implying that when Catholics move into communities (in the West or elsewhere) with highly educated populations, they assimilate a political culture of reformism. Correspondingly, potential League members in such communities may become less active, because they are reasonably content that the victory for reform has already been won. Still, the present data force these interpretations to remain highly tentative.

Decentralization of Decision-Making Structure

As indicated above, the present study was oriented principally toward investigating the causes and consequences of community decision-making patterns. Correspondingly, a larger number of specific propositions had been formulated in this area than in others. Because the more general theoretical considerations concerning each proposition have been treated in detail elsewhere, the presentation here is limited to the propositions and to a discussion of whether the data, shown in Table VIII and Figure III, supported them.[24]

An hypothesis that has been advanced on several occasions is that *the larger the number of inhabitants in*

TABLE VIII

CORRELATIONS AND PATH COEFFICIENTS FOR DECENTRALIZED DECISION-MAKING STRUCTURE

Dependent Variable: Decentralized Decision-Making
Structure: Y

Independent variable	Zero order correlation	Path coefficient
Index of reform government: W	-.548	-.586
Economic diversification: X_4	.347	.477
Industrial activity: X_3	-.008	-.213
Community poverty: X_2	-.031	-.220
Highly educated population: X_5	-.332	-.061
Civic voluntary organization activity: V	-.275	.105
Population size: X_1	.384	.066
Catholic population: X_6	.254	.000

R = .738   Variance explained = 47%

$$Y^a = 11.5429 + \underset{(.000001)}{.0000} \ X_1 - \underset{(.0273)}{.0462} \ X_2 - \underset{(.0219)}{.0393} \ X_3$$

$$+ \underset{(.3751)}{1.3340} \ X_4 - \underset{(.2254)}{.2062} \ X_5 + \underset{(.0015)}{.0012} \ V - \underset{(.1748)}{.6959} \ W$$

[a]Regression coefficients unstandardized; standard errors in parentheses.

FIGURE III

PATH COEFFICIENTS FOR DECENTRALIZED
DECISION-MAKING STRUCTURE

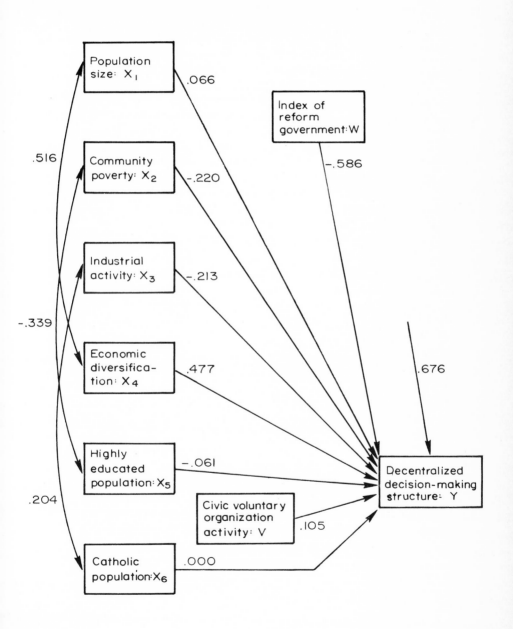

the community, the more decentralized the decision-making structure.[25] But when it was subjected to empirical test, the proposition was not substantiated--to the great dismay, generally, of those forced to present the results.[26] We found that the earlier hypothesis, while showing some support in zero order correlation between the variables of size and decentralization, loses all support in path analysis.

But for most of us who have theorized about population size, the crucial variable is not size alone, but various associated phenomena, with structural differentiation perhaps foremost. With increasing size, more differentiation appears in more community institutions-- economic, political and cultural. Differentiation in the economic sphere has led to the following proposition: *The more diverse the economic structures within a community, the more decentralized the decision-making structure.*[27] Here too, however, empirical support has often been lacking. But once again our findings support the theorized relationship: the more economically diversi- fied communities definitely have more decentralized decision-making structures.

Although differentiation of governmental institu- tions is less clear than differentiation in the economic sector, reform government·could be interpreted as tending toward a less differentiated pattern than the "unre- formed" alternatives of our index. That is, reform government is less differentiated when political institu- tions are considered as a distinct subsystem of the total community. Further, we must recognize that the political subsystem generally, and reform government institutions more specifically, are important mechanisms of integra- tion for the community system. These considerations sug- gest that reform governmental characteristics should lead to more centralized patterns of decisionmaking, as indeed they do.[28] Reform government has the strongest relation- ship with centralization of any variable in the model.

Reform government, in turn, is strongly correlated with a highly educated population. But the zero correlation of education with decentralization is negative. This would seem, at first, to contradict our proposition that *the higher the educational level of community residents, the more pluralistic the decision-making structure*.[29] When the other variables in the model are introduced the negative association disappears, but the proposition is still not supported.

Another variable closely related to a highly educated population is the level of civic voluntary activity. We had postulated that *the greater the density of voluntary organizations in the community, the more decentralized the decision-making structure*.[30] The negative zero order correlation between civic activity and decentralization implies rejection of the proposition, but in the causal model, the relationship--although quite weak--was positive. Highly educated populations thus tend to lead to both reform governments and higher levels of civic activity. But while the first tends toward centralization of decisionmaking, the second may tend toward decentralization. Correspondingly, the general proposition about higher education leading to decentralization is not supported by the present evidence. But the intermediate links in the causal chain need to be specified more precisely before the proposition can be verified or rejected.

A final proposition that we were able to test suggested that *the higher the degree of industrialization in a community, the more decentralized the decision-making structure*.[31] The path coefficient in our model, while not very strong, suggests the opposite relationship. Even if strongly negative, however, the substantive meaning of such a finding would not be self-evident. By international standards, the United States is obviously a highly industrialized country. But the effects of industrialization implied by the proposition do not necessarily make themselves felt in the geographic areas immediately surrounding large industrial

installations. The more indirect consequences of
industrialization--wealth, leisure time, education, more
harmonious social relations--are apparently more important in effecting a decentralized pattern of decisionmaking than industrial activity per se. When these indirect
benefits are separated ecologically from industrial
establishments, the relationship stated in the proposition will no longer hold.

One solution would be to reformulate the proposition
to apply to larger ecological units such as Standard
Metropolitan Statistical Areas or regions. But the differences among communities within the United States are
so small when compared to differences between communities
in the U.S. and in other countries that it seems preferable to test the proposition with comparable data from
communities in less industrialized countries. Several
projects presently under way should make this feasible in
the near future.[32]

Policy Outputs: General Budget and Urban Renewal Expenditures

Until quite recently, neither theoretical nor empirical work on community decisionmaking was concerned with
systematically relating decision-making patterns to
policy outputs.[33] Consequently, the number of propositions in this area was smaller than those predicting patterns of decisionmaking from community structural characteristics.

One basic proposition mentioned in the general formulation above, is that *the more centralized the
decision-making structure, the higher the level of outputs.*[34] But our findings in Table IX and Figure IV, with
regard to both general budget and urban renewal expenditures, were precisely the opposite of those predicted by
this proposition. The fact that certain studies have
supported the proposition suggests that while it is not
necessarily wrong, it is probably incomplete and may
apply only to certain types of decisions.

TABLE IX

CORRELATIONS AND PATH COEFFICIENTS FOR THE
DEPENDENT VARIABLE: URBAN RENEWAL EXPENDITURES

Dependent Variable: Urban Renewal Expenditures: Z_2

Independent variable	Zero order correlation	Path coefficient
Catholic population: X_6	.454	.620
Community poverty: X_2	.136	.527
Population size: X_1	.392	.341
Decentralized decision-making structure: Y	.350	.291
Highly educated population: X_5	-.297	.282
Economic diversification: X_4	.050	-.235
Industrial activity: X_3	.119	.181
Index of reform government: W	-.308	.052
Civic voluntary organization activity: V	-.051	.025
Residual	.....	.708

R = .705   Variance explained = 40%

$$Z_2{}^a = -581.9180 + \underset{(.00006)}{.001} \ X_1 + \underset{(2.2836)}{6.7657} \ X_2 + \underset{(1.5096)}{2.0347} \ X_3$$

$$- \underset{(28.0434)}{40.1232} \ X_4 + \underset{(17.2175)}{22.0305} \ X_5 + \underset{(.9209)}{3.5293} \ X_6 + \underset{(.1061)}{.0169} \ V$$

$$+ \underset{(13.4547)}{3.8038} \ W + \underset{(10.0208)}{17.7491} \ Y$$

[a]Regression coefficients unstandardized; standard errors in parentheses.

FIGURE IV

PATH COEFFICIENTS FOR URBAN
RENEWAL EXPENDITURES

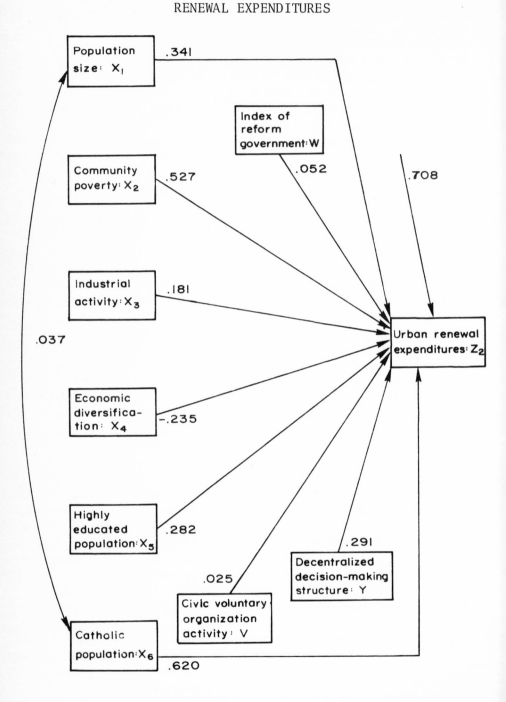

The Concept of Fragility. Earlier studies supporting the proposition have examined such decisions as
fluoridation, school desegregation and urban renewal.
These types of decisions have one characteristic that
apparently differentiates them from our two policy outputs: their *fragility*. Fluoridation studies have continually stressed the difficulty of implementing fluoridation programs after they have come under attack by out-
spoken local community groups. The same is true of
school desegregation. And, if we are to judge from the
earlier case studies of urban renewal programs, and the
quantitative data for the 1950's presented by Hawley,
this would seem to have been the case for urban renewal
as well, at least until recently.[35]

Since an important component of fragility is a program's newness to a community, all things being equal,
fragility should decrease over time. For with time, community residents become increasingly accustomed to the
presence of an activity; the people associated with the
program establish continuing relationships with other
community sectors; initial projects are completed, and
later projects improved. In effect, the program activities become legitimatized. The issues of school desegregation and urban renewal both seem to have become less
fragile than they were a decade ago.

A small but discontented group is much more likely
to be able to find a sympathetic ear among the leadership
in a decentralized community than in a more centralized
community, where the leadership is strong enough to
ignore mild opposition. In the case of a sufficiently
fragile issue, the active opposition of even a small discontented group may delay or halt action. A weak government, or one that requires the participation and active
consent of many supporting groups, is more likely to have
difficulty in carrying out fragile decisions than would a
stronger one. Or, slightly restated, *for fragile decisions, the more centralized the decision-making structure, the higher the level of outputs*.

Insofar as budget construction and more established urban renewal programs may be classified as less fragile decisions, their size should increase with decentralization of the decision-making structure. This we found to be the case.

The Influence of Catholicism. Decentralization of decisionmaking, however, is not the only factor behind budget and urban renewal expenditures in American communities. By far the most influential variable affecting community budget expenditures has been virtually ignored by every major study of which we are aware. This variable is the percent of the community residents who are members of the Roman Catholic Church. The zero order correlation of percent Catholic and budget expenditures was high--.610--but instead of declining in importance when the other variables in the model were introduced, as might be expected, a phenomenally strong path coefficient of .922 was generated. This was the strongest single path coefficient in our entire analysis. The path coefficient from percent Catholic to urban renewal expenditures (Table X) was not quite so impressive, but for budgets it was easily the strongest single path in Figure V. As suggested above, the figures used for religious affiliation have remained unknown to most social scientists although they are not new. That they are somewhat outdated, and necessarily somewhat inexact, should simply lower their correlations with other variables. But that such strong relationships persist even with a crude measure seems remarkable testimony to the importance of a hitherto neglected variable.

How are we to explain these findings? Our first reaction was that there may have been errors in the data, but all figures were checked twice and found to be correct. Our second concern was multicollinearity. We thus examined the zero order correlations between percent Catholic and other variables in order to search out possible strong associations between Catholicism and some other yet unanalyzed factor. Zero order correlations show that communities with large numbers of

TABLE X

CORRELATIONS AND PATH COEFFICIENTS FOR GENERAL BUDGET EXPENDITURES

Dependent Variable: General Budget Expenditures: Z_1

Independent variable	Zero order correlation	Path coefficient
Catholic population: X_6	.610	.922
Index of reform government: W	-.015	.521
Community poverty: X_2	-.100	.422
Economic diversification: X_4	-.045	-.408
Decentralized decision-making structure: Y	.237	.394
Highly educated population: X_5	-.057	.382
Population size: X_1	.310	.369
Civic voluntary organization activity: V	.042	-.126
Industrial activity: X_3	-.062	.097

R = .840   Variance explained = 66%

$$Z_1{}^a = -459.3432 + \underset{(.00003)}{.0001} X_1 + \underset{(1.2558)}{3.8870} X_2 + \underset{(.8301)}{.7850} X_3$$

$$- \underset{(15.4211)}{50.0548} X_4 + \underset{(9.4679)}{21.4175} X_5 + \underset{(.5064)}{3.7679} X_6 - \underset{(.0584)}{.0618} V$$

$$+ \underset{(7.3988)}{27.1004} W + \underset{(5.5105)}{17.2776} Y$$

[a] Regression coefficients unstandardized; standard errors in parentheses.

FIGURE V

PATH COEFFICIENTS FOR GENERAL
BUDGET EXPENDITURES

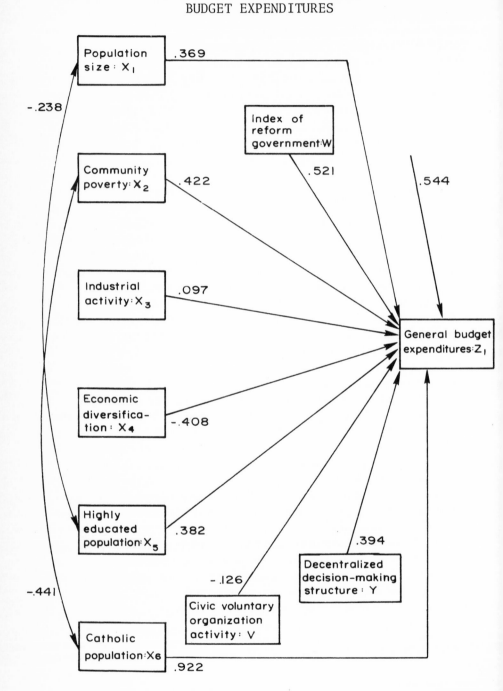

Catholic residents: are often in the Northeast, rarely in the South; have reasonably high population density; are slightly more industrialized than average; have populations that are somewhat less educated and include fewer Protestants than others; but have a relatively small percent of the population with incomes under $3,000. From these findings, one might infer that the Catholic communities tend toward the private-regarding ideal-type of Banfield and Wilson. But although percent Catholic correlated -.425 with reform governmental institutions, strongly Catholic communities tend only slightly toward having a Democratic mayor (.378).

Searching for factors that might be more significant than Catholicism alone in explaining high community expenditures, we introduced into our standard regression model, one or two at a time, these variables of region, population density, various measures of industrial activity, percent of Protestants and Jews in the population, the party of the mayor, and percent Democratic vote in the SMSA in 1960. But none of these factors, to our surprise, seriously decreased the impact of percent Catholic membership. The path coefficient from percent Catholic to budget expenditures never dropped below .680.

Percent Catholic was also quite consistently influential when expenditures on separate budget items were analyzed, instead of the general budget figure. For a total of 23 separate items, it was the most influential single variable for nine items, and second or third most influential for five others. Its influence was virtually zero for six items (highways, highway capital outlays, sewerage, parks and recreation, libraries and general public buildings), and negative for just two (sewerage capital outlays and total utility expenditures). Thus the impact of Catholics on budget expenditures derived not from just a few items, but was found quite consistently on about two-thirds of all budget items.

We then tried to specify what kinds of Catholics were most likely to spend public funds. Much of the literature on ethnic politics suggests that, among Catholics, it is the Irish who have been most consistently involved in politics. But there is little support in the literature for the proposition that Irish Catholics spend more than other national groups.[36]

To specify the relative importance of the various national groups, we computed 16 measures based on eight ethnic sets. These sets included foreign born persons and those with at least one parent born in Ireland, Germany, Poland, Mexico, Italy, Western Europe (United Kingdom, Ireland, Norway, Sweden, Denmark, Switzerland, France), Central Europe (Germany, Poland, Czechoslovakia, Austria and Hungary) and Southern Europe (Greece, Italy, Yugoslavia). The 16 measures were obtained when these eight figures for each community were standardized by dividing by (1) the total number of foreign born and persons with foreign or mixed parents, and (2) the total community population.

Using material from the 1960 census, we were concerned that certain groups, especially the Irish and Germans, would be underrepresented because these figures would fail to reflect the sizeable immigration during the nineteenth century. But although the Irish were probably more underrepresented than most other national groups, they still emerged as the most important one. When the 16 standardized figures were introduced one at a time into our path analysis model for general budget expenditures, in Table XI, only the two Irish figures were significant.[37] With Irish as a percentage of the total community population included in our model, the path coefficient for percent Catholic dropped to .362; the path coefficient for Irish was .501. No other national group or combination of national groups significantly decreased the percent of Catholic relationship. The distinctiveness of Irish Catholics, at least with regard to this issue, suggests that the practice, currently widespread in discussions of city politics, of

TABLE XI

BUDGET EXPENDITURES MODEL WITH IRISH AS A PERCENT OF THE TOTAL COMMUNITY POPULATION INCLUDED

Dependent Variable: General Budget Expenditures: Z_1

Independent variable	Zero order correlation	Path coefficient
Index of reform government: W	-.004	.542
Percent Irish: X_7	.679	.501
Population size: X_1	.330	.365
Percent Catholic: X_6	.573	.362
Economic diversification: X_4	-.007	-.255
Community poverty: X_2	.007	.243
Decentralized decision-making structure: Y	.216	.208
Civic voluntary organization activity: V	-.045	-.047
Highly educated population: X_5	-.166	-.039
Industrial activity: X_3	-.013	.030

R = .848   Variance explained = 65%

$$Z_1^a = 3.5899 + \underset{(.0000)}{.0000} X_1 + \underset{(.0091)}{.0162} X_2 + \underset{(.0059)}{.0018} X_3$$

$$- \underset{(.1075)}{.2257} X_4 - \underset{(.0658)}{.0159} X_5 + \underset{(.0058)}{.0107} X_6 + \underset{(.0618)}{.1779} X_7$$

$$- \underset{(.0667)}{.0260} V + \underset{(.0531)}{.2036} W + \underset{(.0409)}{.0658} Y$$

[a]Regression coefficients unstandardized; standard errors in parentheses.

lumping together persons under such categories as "ethnics," "immigrants," or even "private-regarding" groups, may be highly misleading.

It has been abundantly documented in public opinion studies that Catholics prefer the Democratic over the Republican party, are favorably disposed toward increased governmental activities, and support more extensive welfare state activities.[38] However, the special importance of *Irish* Catholicism in influencing actual policy outcomes has, to our knowledge, not been demonstrated in such striking fashion previously. It is to be hoped that future studies will more often include religious and national background variables in their analysis.

Other Variables. But let us compare our findings somewhat more systematically with those reported by earlier research on community budget expenditures. Probably the most frequently analyzed variables are those associated with wealth. That association is invariably high and positive, whether the expenditures are linked to measures of personal income[39] or to assessed property valuations of communities.[40] These results concur with our .382 path coefficient from education (which is highly associated with measures of wealth) to budget expenditures; the coefficient was .337 from education to urban renewal expenditures. (The path coefficient for median income, when substituted in the model for median education, was lower than for education.)

Most of the rest of our findings, however, differ from earlier research. Studies of suburbs around New York and Philadelphia, for example, showed that measures of the industrial activity of the community were extremely important in explaining governmental expenditure levels.[41] Our findings suggest that the tendency of one community to spend more than others nearby (by taxing its industries) is more a specifically suburban phenomenon. Various measures of industrial activity--

the per capita number of manufacturing establishments
with more than 20 employees, per capita value added by
manufacturing, percent of industrial establishments with
20 or more employees--were introduced one at a time into
our model, but all were of minimal importance.

Hawley observed several years ago that the proportion of the SMSA population residing in the central city
was more important in predicting budget expenditures
than the actual city population, and Brazer reported the
same relationship for large American cities.[42] This
proportion was not important for our sample, however,
presumably because we included more small and independent communities.

The other variables that exercised some influence
on budget expenditures were reform government (positively), economic diversification (negatively), the size
of the poverty sector (positively), and the total population size (positively). Voluntary organization
activity, however, showed no impact on budget or urban
renewal expenditures. Apropos of the explanatory
importance of many of our noneconomic variables, some
of the recent studies by economists and economics-
oriented political scientists would be more useful if
they considered such noneconomic variables more systematically.[43]

CONCLUSION

Without following Comte too closely, we may suggest that the study of community decisionmaking has
developed in three stages. After a power elitist stage
inspired by Hunter and Mills, and a pluralist stage
influenced by Dahl, a comparative stage now seems to
be in the offing. This third phase poses not just new
questions, but new types of questions. No longer
restricted to finding Who Governs?, the query is
extended to include Who Governs, Where, When, and With
What Effects? A growing body of propositions specifying

answers to these questions under varying conditions is inspired by theoretical advances in several substantive areas, as well as by empirical decision-making studies employing a broad variety of methods. Further, if propositions are to be verified, reformulated, or rejected, more rigorous procedures must be utilized to "test" them, particularly by sorting out interrelationships among many variables within a reasonably large number of communities. This paper points in that new direction in its systematic investigation of decision-making in 51 communities of varying sizes. The data collected by methods described earlier enabled us to test a series of previously formulated propositions relating structure and structural characteristics to decision-making patterns and outputs in these communities.

These findings, on the whole, supported our general formulation: *The greater the horizontal and vertical differentiation in a social system, the greater the differentiation between potential elites and the more decentralized the decision-making structure. Without the establishment of integrative mechanisms, this leads to less coordination between sectors and a lower level of outputs.*

Horizontal differentiation of basic community structures was best reflected in the economic sphere in *economic diversification* and to some extent in the political sphere in the *index of reform government*.

Differentiation between potential elites, although not measured directly, was to some extent indicated by active *civic voluntary associations*. These in turn reflected the degree of development of a potential elite group outside of and in addition to others formally involved in community decisionmaking.

Decentralized decisionmaking was positively associated with *economic diversification* and (very slightly) active *civic voluntary associations*, and negatively

associated with the *index of reform government*. All of
these relationships were consistent with our reasoning
that the greater the structural support for a plurality
of potential elites, the more decentralized the decision-
making structure.

Our best indicator of the strength of *community
integrative mechanisms* was the *index of reform government*, which tended to lead to higher outputs.

Specification and revision of the general formulation seemed most necessary in the relationship of the
antecedent variables to the *level of outputs*. In contrast to our expectations, *decentralization of decision-
making* was positively associated with both *budget expenditures* and *urban renewal expenditures*. We suggested
one alternative interpretation of this finding, but further study of community outputs is needed before we can
formulate more precise propositions relating community
characteristics to various types of community outputs.
It is necessary here, as with the other causal mechanisms suggested, to specify the actual content and
structure of the processes involved, using all kinds of
procedures.

At this point we may return to the highly detailed
case study, which can once more perform an indispensable
function. Content analysis and attitude questionnaires
can also be profitably employed to relate political cultural variables to the largely structural variables used
in our model. In this regard, analysis of social and
cultural characteristics of community leaders should be
especially profitable. Finally, replication of these
findings is needed, both in smaller and larger American
communities, and in foreign societies marked by differing structural and cultural patterns of local community
decisionmaking. Only in this way will it be possible to
generate and verify a more general theory of decision-
making.

NOTES

Author's comment: This paper is a revised and expanded version of an article published in *American Sociological Review*, 33(4): 576-593 (1968).

I am grateful to Harold Bloom, William Kornblum and David Monsees for assistance in data processing, and to Leo A. Goodman, Robert W. Hodge, Jack Sawyer, Joe L. Spaeth and Donald B. Treiman for suggestions on statistical matters.

General support for the research leading to this report was generously provided by the McNeil Foundation of Philadelphia and the National Science Foundation. Support for preparation of the manuscript was made available by the Social Science Research Committee of the University of Chicago and the American-Yugoslav Project in Urban and Regional Planning Studies in Ljubljana.

This is research paper #5 of the Comparative Study of Community Decision-Making, supported by grant GS-1904 from the National Science Foundation.

[1] Cf. Terry N. Clark, "Power and Community Structure: Who Governs, Where, and When?" *The Sociological Quarterly*, 8(3): 291-316 (1967) and the works cited there.

[2] See Clark, ibid.

[3] Peter H. Rossi, "Power and Community Structure," in Terry N. Clark, ed., *Community Structure and Decision-Making: Comparative Analyses* (San Francisco: Chandler, 1968), pp. 129-138.

[4] Robert Presthus, *Men at the Top* (New York: Oxford University Press, 1964); Robert E. Agger et al., *The Rulers and the Ruled* (New York: John Wiley and Sons, 1964); Oliver P. Williams and Charles R. Adrian, *Four Cities* (Philadelphia: University of Pennsylvania Press, 1963).

[5]Terry N. Clark et al., "Discipline, Method, Community Structure and Decision-Making: The Role and Limitations of the Sociology of Knowledge," *The American Sociologist*, 3(3): 214-217 (1968); Claire W. Gilbert, "Community Power and Decision-Making: A Quantitative Examination of Previous Research," in Clark, *Community Structure*, pp. 139-156; John Walton, "Differential Patterns of Community Power Structure: An Explanation Based on Interdependence," also in Clark, *Community Structure*, pp. 441-459; and John Walton "Substance and Artifact: The Current Status of Research on Community Power Structure," *American Journal of Sociology*, 71(4): 430-438 (1966).

[6]The background history is contained in Clark, *Community Structure*, Chapter 22, and in Peter H. Rossi and Robert L. Crain, "The NORC Permanent Community Sample," *Public Opinion Quarterly*, 32(2): 261-272 (1968).

[7]Various measures of reliability and validity are presently being prepared, and will be reported in subsequent papers.

[8]Cf. the theoretical discussions in Clark, *Community Structure*, Chapter 3, "The Concept of Power," and Theodore J. Lowi, "American Business, Public Policy, Case Studies, and Political Theory," *World Politics*, 16(4): 677-715 (1964).

[9]We understand by *decision-making structure* the patterned distribution of *influence* exercised in a community, in contrast to the patterned distribution of *resources*, which is better referred to as a *power-structure*. Cf. Clark, *Community Structure*, Chapter 3.

[10]If there were more than two "sides" to an issue, the third (or fourth) side was treated as a second (or third) distinct "opponent."

[11]Cf. Robert A. Dahl, *Who Governs?* (New Haven: Yale University Press, 1961); Presthus, *Men at the Top*; and Terry N. Clark, "The Concept of Power: Some Overemphasized and Underrecognized Dimensions," *Southwestern Social Science Quarterly*, 48(3): 271-286 (1967).

[12]Ruth Moser, a University of Chicago graduate student, experimented with alternative weighting schemes as part of the comparative study. See her "Correlates of Decision-Making in Eighteen New England Communities," unpublished M.A. thesis, Department of Sociology, University of Chicago, 1967.

[13]Clark, "Power and Community Structure," note 1 above.

[14]Clark, *Community Structure*, Chapter 5, "Community Structure and Decision-Making." See note 3 above.

[15]The source for information about each variable is indicated under Table II, except for the governmental characteristics, taken from *The Municipal Yearbook 1966* (Chicago: International City Managers Association, 1966).

[16]See Howard J. Nelson, "A Service Classification of American Cities," *Economic Geography*, 31(3): 189-210 (1955). A dummy variable format was used when correlating qualitative with quantitative variables. Cf. N.R. Draper and H. Smith, *Applied Regression Analysis* (New York: John Wiley and Sons, 1966).

[17]Edward C. Banfield and James Q. Wilson, *City Politics* (Cambridge: Harvard University Press, 1965); Charles R. Adrian and Charles Press, *Governing Urban America* (New York: McGraw-Hill, 1968). See especially Chapter 8.

[18]This same procedure was used by Lineberry and Fowler, but they included commission government as a reform characteristic. See Robert L. Lineberry and Edmund P. Fowler, "Reformism and Public Policies in American Cities," *American Political Science Review*, 61(3): 701-716 (1967). In a personal communication, Lineberry agreed that our weighting scheme is probably more appropriate.

[19]Path analysis, although developed by the geneticist Sewall Wright in the 1920's, has been utilized only seldom as a statistical technique. The work of Simon and Blalock stimulated interest in causal models, while a recent article by Duncan has brought the path analysis used in genetics to the attention of contemporary

sociologists. Raymond Boudon's outstanding study to date is the most thorough treatment of path analysis and its relationships to more traditional statistical procedures. With the increasing concern in the social sciences for specifically causal models, and the ease of data processing made possible by high speed computers, path analysis may well become widely used in the near future. See Herbert A. Simon, *Models of Man: Social and National* (New York: John Wiley and Sons, 1957); Hubert M. Blalock, *Causal Inferences in Non-Experimental Research* (Chapel Hill: University of North Carolina Press, 1964); Raymond Boudon, *L'analyse mathématique des faits sociaux* (Paris: Plon, 1967); and Otis Dudley Duncan, "Path Analysis: Sociological Examples," *American Journal of Sociology*, 72(1): 1-16 (1966).

[20] Figures I through V, when superimposed upon one another, constitute a complete path analysis diagram with all traditional elements included. The difficulties of reading such a complex diagram led us to break it down into five separate parts, each of which corresponds to a single dependent variable.

Each of the five tables also contains the corresponding regression equation, including the intercept, the unstandardized regression coefficients for each variable, and (in parentheses) the standard error of each regression coefficient. Linear least squares regression was used in every case except for ethnicity, for only a few variables were sufficiently skewed to justify transformation. However, see footnote 37 below.

[21] There are one or two cases that follow in which the causal sequence is not as clear-cut as indicated by the path analysis diagrams. While fully recognizing this point, we felt that it was valuable to attempt causal statements wherever possible, instead of speaking merely in terms of associations. Our interpretations may then be more directly validated or revised by future studies.

[22] Cf. Murray Hausknecht, *The Joiners: A Sociological Description of Voluntary Association Membership in the United States* (New York: Bedminster Press, 1962).

[23] Robert Alford and Harry Scoble, "Political and Socio-Economic Characteristics of American Cities," *The Municipal Yearbook 1965* (Chicago: International City Managers Association, 1965), pp. 82-97; John H. Kessel, "Government Structure and Political Environment: A Statistical Note About American Cities," *American Political Science Review*, 56: 615-620 (September 1962); Raymond E. Wolfinger and John Osgood Field, "Political Ethos and the Structure of City Government," in Clark, *Community Structure*, pp. 159-195 (note 3 above); and Lineberry and Fowler, note 18 above.

[24] For the theoretical considerations, see Clark, *Community Structure*.

[25] For documentation, see Clark, "Power and Community Structure" (note 1 above), proposition 1.

[26] Clark, *Community Structure*, pp. 96ff.

[27] Clark, ibid., p. 102.

[28] See Clark, ibid., pp. 107ff., for further discussion.

[29] Clark, ibid., p. 119.

[30] Clark, ibid., p. 115.

[31] Clark, ibid., p. 107.

[32] Clark, ibid., Chapter 22, "Present and Future Research on Community Decision-Making: The Problem of Comparability."

[33] See, however, the articles in Section VII of Clark, ibid.

[34] Some support exists for this proposition. See Amos H. Hawley, "Community Power and Urban Renewal Success," pp. 393-405, in Clark, *Community Structure*; Donald B. Rosenthal and Robert L. Crain, "Structure and Values in Local Political Systems: The Case of Fluoridation Decisions," pp. 215-242, in Clark, *Community Structure*; and Clark, *Community Structure*, pp. 92ff.

[35] See the Hawley article in Clark, *Community Structure*.

[36] Harold F. Gosnell, *Machine Politics: Chicago Model*, 2d ed. (Chicago: University of Chicago Press, 1968); Nathan Glazer and Daniel P. Moynihan, *Beyond the Melting Pot: The Negroes, Puerto Ricans, Jews, Italians, and Irish of New York City* (Cambridge: The M.I.T. Press, 1963); and Edward M. Levine, *The Irish and Irish Politicians: A Study of Cultural and Social Alienation* (Notre Dame: University of Notre Dame Press, 1966).

[37] Because the distributions for several variables were slightly skewed, a natural logarithmic transformation was used for 13 of the nationality variables. In Table XI the natural logarithms of variables X_6, V, and Z_2 were used.

[38] Angus Campbell et al., *The American Voter* (New York: John Wiley and Sons, 1964); Philip E. Converse, "Religion and Politics: The 1960 Elections," in Angus Campbell et al., *Elections and the Political Order* (New York: John Wiley and Sons, 1966), pp. 96-124; and Gerhard Lenski, *The Religious Factor* (Garden City, N.Y.: Doubleday-Anchor, 1961), pp. 152-154.

[39] Harvey Elliot Brazer, *City Expenditures in the United States* (New York: National Bureau of Economic Research, 1959); Alan Campbell and Seymour Sacks, *Metropolitan America* (New York: Free Press, 1967); and Seymour Sacks and William F. Hellmuth, Jr., *Financing Government in a Metropolitan Area: The Cleveland Experience* (New York: Free Press, 1961).

[40] Sacks and Hellmuth, ibid.; John C. Bollens, ed., *Exploring the Metropolitan Community* (Berkeley and Los Angeles: University of California Press, 1961); Glenn W. Fisher and Robert P. Fairbanks, *Illinois Municipal Finance: A Political and Economic Analysis* (Urbana: University of Illinois Press, 1968); Stanley Scott and Edward L. Feder, *Factors Associated with Variations in Municipal Expenditure Levels* (Berkeley: Bureau of Public Administration, University of California, 1957).

[41] Robert C. Wood, *1400 Governments: The Political Economy of the New York Metropolitan Region* (New York:

Doubleday-Anchor, 1964); Oliver P. Williams et al., *Suburban Differences and Metropolitan Policies* (Philadelphia: University of Pennsylvania Press, 1965).

[42] See Brazer, *City Expenditures* (note 39 above), and Amos H. Hawley, "Metropolitan Population and Municipal Government Expenditures in Central Cities," *Journal of Social Issues*, 7(1-2): 100-108 (1951).

[43] This includes many studies in the *National Tax Journal*, as well as the work of Dye and Sharkansky.

The Application of Computers to Community Power Study

by FLOYD HUNTER

Social Science Research and Development

CONTENTS

Although I know we are going to have an opportunity to speak to each other later, I can't help remarking on two or three things said by earlier speakers. First, I believe that the great rash of case studies in recent years is partly due to the fact that the study of the individual community is a relatively simple and inexpensive process, whereas the study of the national system is expensive and very time consuming.

Second, I think that one of the difficulties in some of the studies is measuring power, asking how much power, treating it as a "commodity" rather than as a "process." Power is a process, and community power is related in this world of ours to national systems of power. For instance, one wants to move goods and services across distances. You define power, then, by its function. And when it is defined by its function, you recognize that it is really concerned with the maintenance of order and national systems.

Finally, some of you know that although a good deal of my work has been strongly criticized by any number of scholars, I have generally refused to engage in polemical discussions about the criticisms. I still refuse to do so. As I look over the studies, I think some of the criticisms are valid, but many of them are really political in nature. I think a good deal of the language I read about pluralism, for example, is baloney. Some people are simply apologists for a highly centralized nationalistic system that does some pretty sorry things around the nation and around the world.

THE STUDY OF ECONOMIC POWER STRUCTURES

I think the best answer to questions concerning community power studies is to make another study, so I want to take a few minutes to talk about a study that my company and I have been making for the last two years for the Department of Commerce's Economic Development Administration. The study deals with economic power structures and the process of capital development in a submetropolitan community, Oakland, California. About 20 of us were involved in the study--economists, sociologists, anthropologists and computer scientists. We figured that we live in a capitalistic society, and one important thing that a capitalistic society does is develop capital resources. So who are the people involved in this important activity, and how are they related to each other?

Our underlying questions, the primary analytical questions on which the study is focused, are: (1) Who are the economic decisionmakers for Oakland, inside and outside the community, from the national structure on down? (2) How do they relate to one another? (3) How do they relate to other decisionmakers in Oakland? (4) What are their goals in trying to socially, politically and economically rebuild portions of the community? (5) How valid were their decisions regarding the community's problem of unemployment?

THE RESEARCH PLAN

To pursue these questions, we worked up a research plan that consisted of five elements. First was the construction of lists of power nominees to be tested in subsequent analysis. Second was the construction of matrices of corporate directors and community leaders. Third was the administration of a unit questionnaire to a self-generating sample and to subsamples. Fourth, computer matrices analysis was used to manipulate the data generated in the first three steps. Finally, economic data were analyzed with reference to power decisions. The use of the computer matrices contains elements that may be particularly useful to others committed to the task of analyzing data related to complex social structures.

In our case, the utilization of computer systems techniques and controls enabled the researchers to

(a) derive empirically a system of interaction, and (b) construct a central pool of data related to the purposes of such interaction. This form of analysis can be undertaken by utilizing the relevant aspects of previous studies or approaches (reputational, positional or decisional) and coordinating the data and the data gathering, a mechanism that uses matrix systems analysis.

The data system is based on the following operational procedures. First, a unit questionnaire was administered to all interviewees. We skipped the usual two-step approach, which you may recall from the earlier Atlanta study. Instead, we went to various social organizations and gathered reputational nominations, then went to the nominees and asked them what they did, what projects they were related to, and so forth. There has been considerable confusion in the literature about reputational studies not using projects and issues. In fact, I used them from the first. But in this particular study, because we had the computer at our command, we were able to eliminate the judges and thereby some of the criticism of the earlier methods. But I think we came out in about the same place.

After this, we conducted the initial round of interviews, which determined the population from which subsequent interviewees were chosen. The sample was thus self-generating. Respondents for subsequent rounds of interviews were selected through periodic processing of available data. Although the data could have been processed daily, it was found that data did not accumulate rapidly enough to make such frequent processing practical. The data system and subsequent analysis system were thus based upon utilizing and expanding the data pool and matrix analysis of connections among persons, positions and projects. The self-generating sample was finally tested by comparing and contrasting it with a series of population subsamples. Data related to power nominees, matrices and corporate leaders were also gathered in the Oakland study, but will not be discussed at present. The success of the self-generating sample and the use of matrix analysis meant, as I said before, that the use of judges for preliminary community power nominations was not necessary.

The so-called unit questionnaire, which inquired about the interpersonal relationships involved in economic power decisions, was administered to the self-generating sample; results were then coded and processed for analysis and evaluation. The questionnaire was so designed that it could, with slight modifications, be administered to top influentials, ghetto residents, or economic and political elites, wherever they might reside. After four interviews had been completed, names mentioned by the first four respondents became the next interviewees. Each was selected on the quantitative basis of the number of leadership nominations received. At no time during the initial four interviews were arbitrary nominations made by the research staff.

Matrix analysis also made it possible to detect hidden leaders by manipulating or squaring the nominations matrix. Subsystems of leadership within the total structure were uncovered by reordering the matrix and squaring it to correspond with the attribute and attitude rankings of nominators. Closure within the system and subsystems was demonstrated. Each person interviewed generated some nonzero entries in the left-hand matrix of persons interviewed and some additional entries to the right-hand matrix of persons who were yet to be interviewed. When all the nominees receiving three or more nominations had been interviewed, the number of additional entries in the right-hand submatrix became extremely small.

THE ADVANTAGES OF COMPUTERS IN COMMUNITY POWER RESEARCH

Our Oakland study involved two major refinements compared to our earlier method of conducting power structure studies. First, the sample interviewed was self-generating rather than preselected. Second, both the processes of data gathering and the data analysis were designed around the use of computers. The use of the computer in both the sample and data analysis stages of the study was made possible through the use of matrices, meaning that the data could be manipulated, rather than simply being put forward in visible graphs and sociograms.

Several special advantages resulted from this method of study. First, it was possible to process the data from several hundred questionnaires rapidly. Second, data analysis could proceed before the whole study or interviewing process was completed, and the results of this intermediate analysis could be used as a guide in conducting subsequent interviews. Third, during the analysis stage, a large number of data and manipulating processes could be conducted in a short period of time.

In the first study I made, I didn't have the computer and I didn't have people helping me, so I cut my data into little pieces, names of people and projects, and spread them out on a big table, three or four times as long as this one before us. Then I'd run from one end of the table to another, trying to get cliques. The computer is very helpful along these lines. I would suggest that the ideal procedure is (1) to define how the components of the social system are expected to interact; (2) to search for mathematical analogues of these components and interactions; (3) to perform the data manipulation suggested by these mathematical analogues; and (4) to translate the results into sociological interpretations.

CONCLUSION

Let me summarize quickly what we tried to do in studying power and capitalization processes in Oakland: (1) delineate the economy of the submetropolitan community; (2) identify policy-making personnel in the regional, federal and local power structures, as well as in the economic power structures; (3) relate power structures to specific economic policy decisions; and (4) test the validity--in terms of extent and effectiveness--of decisions aimed at reducing chronic unemployment and underemployment.

Since I'm talking about methodology here, I can't go into details of what we found substantively. But if any of you are interested in talking about what we found, I would be glad to talk to you informally at any point and answer questions. Here I can merely sketch what we learned. We found, first, that Oakland, like every other city in the land, had a power structure. Second, the IBM machine found a civic machine that moved rapidly to closure. In other words, there is a small group of public and private politicans who are always present to keep the machine on the right tracks. Third, the processes of inclusion and exclusion leave far too many people out, and leave far too much undone. Fourth, the local power structure relates to a number of forces in the larger metropolitan community and in the national power structure.

Finally, we spent far too much money--$140,000--to learn this all over again. The first study cost $600. From now on, we will not ask the redundant question "Is there a power structure?" Instead, we will ask "Who is in the power structure? With whom do they link up? About what? and, Are their objectives remotely worthwhile, socially and politically?"

Where the Pluralists Went Wrong

by HARRY M. SCOBLE

University of California, Los Angeles

CONTENTS

INTRODUCTION

One of the freedoms associated with giving a panel paper at a professional meeting or participating in a special research seminar is that one need not waste time or space on the scholastic formalisms of the *American Political Science Review* format or the footnote rigidities of the University of Chicago's *Manual of Style*. At least in the present case, I intend to indulge myself in precisely that freedom or luxury. While I shall discuss a large number of authors, I will limit myself to minimal formal identification of their works.

I have also chosen to give my remarks a title-- "Where The Pluralists Went Wrong." Perhaps I am guilty of conceit. At the least, I readily admit that I am guilty of ulterior motives in choosing this particular title. First, I intend to be an *agent provocateur*, to deliberately exaggerate for the purpose of emphasis. By doing this I hope to stimulate political scientists to further research on power distribution. What other central focus could a confessedly unreconstructed Lasswellian have?

But I admit a second kind of guilt as well: there is, in fact, no single "school" that can legitimately be identified as "pluralist." Indeed, our colleagues among the political philosophers would render us inestimable aid and comfort if they would undertake the taxonomic task of developing usable typologies of pluralism. Thus by "pluralists" I mean specifically the "Yale community politics" scholars--Robert A. Dahl and his students Nelson W. Polsby and Raymond E. Wolfinger. To this group of pluralists I shall add others in the course of my talk.

Let me add also that I am disturbed by two tendencies that I perceive in the political science profession. First, since 1961, when Robert A. Dahl won this

profession's highest literary and research award--the
Woodrow Wilson Award--for the publication of his study
of New Haven, Connecticut, I have perceived a tendency to
put *Who Governs?* on the bookshelf alongside Bryce,
de Tocqueville and other classics. It is often unread,
rarely studied, never questioned.[1] Related to this is
the noncumulative nature of the research literature on
community political systems, at least among political
scientists. Neither Dahl, nor Polsby, nor Wolfinger has
returned to the field for additional research. Indeed,
Who Governs? differs from most social science research
monographs in its unique lack of concern for the future.
One finds no discussion of the new research that might be
done, similar to that in the Appendix of *The Rulers and
the Ruled*, by Robert E. Agger et al. Nor is concern
shown for the policy implications of the study, as in the
concluding chapter of Donald R. Matthews' *The Social
Backgrounds of Political Decision-Makers*.[2]

Second, there has been a tendency to engage in an
unprofessional and unbecoming personal vendetta against
the sociologists of community power, particularly Floyd
Hunter. This is both unfair to Hunter and demeaning to
political scientists. First, Hunter's publication of
Community Power Structure in 1953 did, in fact, reinvig-
orate one of the deadest branches of political science.
Lawrence Herson's two survey articles in the *American
Political Science Review* demonstrated this beneficial
stimulus.

Third, the one effort by a political scientist to
replicate (and probably also to refute) Hunter's Atlanta,
Georgia, findings about the "reputed" power of economic
dominants has left us with ambiguous results. I refer,
of course, to M. Kent Jennings' *Community Influentials*,
a restudy of Atlanta, which is marred by peculiar techniques in typecasting and the allocation of various
leadership categories. Consequently Jennings' study
cannot be interpreted as refuting Hunter's original findings. More recently, to my knowledge, no political scientist has attempted to refute Hunter's conclusions about
Oakland, California (as published in *Ramparts*, 1967). In

short, political scientists may have to learn to live with the possibility that there is a true plurality of local power structure types, including one where economic power indeed controls.

But beyond that, I am arguing that we political scientists should stop the endless rehashing of old charges occasionally spiced with gratuitous personal abuse. Our professional answer should be more, better and comparative research to determine factually whether Hunter was right, partly right, or wrong in his conclusions. If we cannot or will not do that, let us be silent.

As my final introductory comment, let me make it clear that I do not intend to restate the old complaints against *Who Governs?* and the "Yale pluralist school" as made in the articles and reviews of William D'Antonio, Floyd Hunter, Hugh Douglas Price or Morton S. Baratz and Peter Bachrach. My purpose is the much more limited one of making us conscious of *new* problems posed by *Who Governs?* and the Yale community pluralists. Thus I intend to raise 11 new points that I hope will prove useful in stimulating further research.

CITY POLITICS AND NATIONAL POLICIES

No matter how good, i.e., valid and reliable, the study of a particular American community may be, it does not permit us to draw any inferences about the distribution of political power in the national polity. Such inferences are impermissible despite Dahl's obvious desire in the latter portion of *Who Governs?* to generalize from New Haven to the entire national system. At the psychological level, for example, community identification is in no way analogous to national citizenship, identity and commitment. More importantly, the local community in no way engages in policy with an impact on the individual comparable to that of the Selective Service System or foreign-military policy.

Indeed, it is my impression that pluralists have largely ignored critical areas of national policy. We lack research, for example, on the domestic political impact of corporate mergers and the growth of "conglomerates"; on the influence of U.S. corporate investments overseas on our foreign policy; on the impact of "the military-industrial-congressional-labor-union complex" on the federal budget and thus on regional growth. Perhaps Floyd Hunter's *Top Leadership, USA* will be rediscovered and reevaluated by political scientists. Or perhaps G. William Domhoff's *Who Rules America?*, his essay on "Who Made Foreign Policy, 1945-1963?" and James Rosenau's recent volume on *The Domestic Sources of Foreign Policy* will have the same desirable effect on these relatively neglected questions as Hunter's work did in 1953.

But let me return to my main theme, that there is a curious disjunction in which the "power elitists'" discussion of essentially national politics and policies has been attacked by the more recent pluralists with evidence drawn from local arenas. For the purposes of argument, let us assume that the pluralists are entirely correct about the local community. It is still possible that American local politics, however pluralistic, has little relevance to the major policies impinging upon the lives of most Americans.

Andrew Hacker, for one, has suggested that the term "power elite" ought to be used in a more sophisticated manner. It is possible, he notes, that an elite perceives certain problems as wholly irrelevant to its interests. These may include "major" local issues or such national questions as civil rights for Negroes. Thus the power elite leaves the consideration and control of these problems to others, who invoke other decision-making rules and produce other outcomes. But regardless of this possibility, I think the first point is valid: the local community is not identical with the national polity and, therefore, no matter how good our studies of the former, they do not permit us to reach any firm judgments about the latter.

CONTROVERSIAL AND NONCONTROVERSIAL ISSUES

Second, *Who Governs?* focuses solely upon controversial decisions and issues. Others have already noted the lack of a satisfactory rationale for selecting controversies. While it is not my intent to restate their criticisms, I think their complaints are valid: we need good descriptive "maps" of decisions, issues and nondecisions in order to avail ourselves of the scientific contribution inherent in probability sampling.[3]

Here I wish to point out one of the consequences of focusing on controversies: noncontroversies are ignored even though they may involve significant allocations of value in the Lasswellian and Eastonian senses. For example, we may ask ourselves whether the best (new or old) public school teachers are assigned to the worst ghetto schools in our urban centers. A strong argument could be made that this is necessary and desirable, yet my impression--from New Haven, New York, Chicago and Los Angeles--is that the opposite occurs. Similarly, political scientists might study the "opportunity structure" for policemen to determine where the individual policeman is assigned as he gains tenure and presumably proficiency in human relations. "Police recruit" standards are also worthy of attention. Because they now usually specify both minimum height and minimum weight, the standards can produce a situation (both unintended and undesired) in which a city finds itself without policemen from minority groups. This occurred in Chicago in 1966. There was a major riot in the Puerto Rican community, but there were few Puerto Rican policemen who could help deal with the situation.

Finally, we might investigate something as simple as the decision to operate a social welfare agency on a nine-to-five, five-days-a-week basis. Middle-class values and perspectives are involved, as is bureaucratic efficiency. These factors may unconsciously preclude consideration of the possibility that personal problems and crises often come to a head at nighttime with time to drink, or on weekends with time to think. Nor should

we overlook the development of new public services or the
location of new school buildings or other public facilities, primarily in the suburban fringe areas. In short,
I am arguing that these routine decisions involve significant allocations of value, and that they may also
provide some explanation of the demonstrated restlessness
of Black and poor citizens since 1964.

SYMBOLIC FUNCTIONS OF POLITICS

For the third item in my bill of indictment, I suggest that political scientists, and perhaps also sociologists, have ignored the symbolic functions of local politics. Murray Edelman has recently done a superior job in
delineating the role and significance of symbolism in
American national politics. We also have Gusfield's
Symbolic Crusade and Merelman's general treatment of "The
Dramaturgy of Politics" in the 1968 *American Sociological
Review*. The problem of "disaggregating" this analysis to
the state or local level, however, remains to be investigated. We have Thomas Anton's analysis of a state's budgets in the *Midwest Journal of Political Science* and
Norton Long's characterization of municipal master plans
as "civic New Year's resolutions." Yet little has been
done beyond this, perhaps because we academics, striving
to be rational ourselves, impute too much rationality to
our fellows. We ignore how much their lives are guided
(and guarded?) by magic and ritual, as well as how
political symbolism induces political quiescence.

As examples, David Riesman and Nathan Glazer sought
some time ago to measure the "quality" of electoral participation. The late V.O. Key, Jr. attempted to defend
The Responsible Electorate, but he was relatively unper-
suasive. The question should be further pursued for, at
local or national levels, there is such an animal as the
"ritualistic voter," utterly uninformed, utterly uninter-
ested, utterly inactive, except for the simple act of
voting itself. We should study such voters in terms of
causes and consequences, and perhaps also in terms of
remedial policies.

At another level, we ought to view municipal institutions and policies with a very skeptical eye. Who in fact gets on the local Board of Zoning Appeals and who benefits from the decisions it makes? Why do city or county human relations commissions tend to be powerless PR devices? Why do we have such conflict-of-interest strictures governing judges and executives, but not legislators? If "open occupancy" legislation exists, is it meaningful, given the salary structure and the overall economic system?

More specifically, following the Watts riot or rebellion, I sought to evaluate "special blue-ribbon study commissions" in precisely these terms and I came to the conclusion that their primary political function was largely symbolic.[4]

THE REPUTATIONAL TECHNIQUE

Fourth, the pluralists have maligned the reputational technique in local political studies, indicating that at best it produces only a measure of potential power. It seems to me that there are at least four different levels of response to make to this charge. To begin with, one might simply reassert (perhaps not fully verbatim) W.I. Thomas' claim that "what men believe is real, is real in its consequences." That is, if men believe there is a power structure with a narrow elite at the top, they will act accordingly and such a power structure will come into being, i.e., potential power will become actual power. In a sense, we enter the thicket of Carl J. Friedrich's "law of anticipated reaction," with which power analysts have had so much difficulty in coming to grips.[5]

Next, at a more empirical level, one might simply cite Robert Presthus' *Men At The Top* and Linton Freeman's studies of political leadership in Syracuse, New York. Using comparative methodology, both conclude that the "decision event reconstruction" method preferred by

political scientists apparently does not identify all
those with power and/or influence in such decisions.
This is a point to which I shall return later.

Futher, if the social stratification system is an
allocative mechanism and control process, then it is
useful to identify those with high prestige, esteem,
status--i.e., with reputation--as potential and probable
high political actors. This, however, verges on my criticism of the pluralists' treatment of social class, a
topic I will treat in more detail below.

Finally, and perhaps most importantly, despite all
our criticisms, political scientists themselves make use
of a modified form of the reputational technique. Our
data derive primarily, and necessarily, from key informants' reports about themselves and about other people.
Even though a situational context of controversies has
been specified, much of the original bill of particulars
against reputationalism remains relevant. However
detailed the situational context, we are still dealing
with reputations for potential power whenever we move
from descriptions of recent past history to statements
and projections about the future of our communities.

FORMAL POLITICAL STRUCTURES

A fifth in the list of conceptual shortcomings is
found less often among political scientists than among
the political sociologists of community power. Perhaps
as an unintended consequence of the behavioral revolution, we political scientists have increasingly ignored
formal structures and institutions. As an example,
Robert Alford notes that the New Haven City Council, with
33 members, is second in size only to Chicago's. Perhaps this indicates that it is easier for a mayor to control local politics when he deals with a large city council than when he faces a small one.

POLITICAL CONTRIBUTIONS

Sixth, the pluralistic literature has concentrated on general elections and has largely ignored primary elections and the nomination process. Furthermore, the literature tends to ignore the influence of money on political choice. Most of what we do know involves national and presidential, rather than local level politics. However, recent scandals and indictments in Los Angeles suggest that winning nominations or elections may be expensive in terms not only of time-investments, but also of actual cash.

We do have some material available. Since publication of Alexander Heard's *The Costs of Democracy*, the Citizens' Research Foundation headed by Herbert Alexander has provided quantities of information on the topic. The quadrennial presidential studies by the University of Michigan's Survey Research Center add still further detail concerning the frequency of political contributions, however small. Yet we have not faced the problem of evaluating the impact of money on politics. Even such an avowed pluralist as Arnold M. Rose concedes, in *The Power Structure*, that neglect of the probable role of "political money" poses serious difficulties for the pluralistic interpretation.

Perhaps the problem is more difficult to study than presidential voting, but the topics we investigate should not be dictated by the existence or nonexistence of a sophisticated methodological apparatus.

THE ANALYSIS OF SOCIAL CLASS

Seventh, as I indicated earlier, I believe that the social background analyses contained in the pluralistic literature are inadequate in several respects. First, Dahl quietly dismisses 15 of his 50 policy activists for the simple reason that they are collectivities and interacting social aggregates rather than individuals. Yet it would seem that a pluralism-oriented political scientist

would want to make use of interest group pluralism, so as
to provide the most comprehensive possible framework of
analysis. I think we would all agree that a business
corporation such as a bank, department store or the
Southern New England Bell Telephone Company may be a significant political interest group at the local level.[6]

Next, the pluralists implicitly assume that diversity in social origin has important political consequences. That is, Dahl shows that 28 of his 35 individual policy-agents were neither Social nor Economic
Notables. Further, they all represented diverse religio-
ethnic groups. The implication is quite clear: upward
social mobility is common in American society and has
important political consequences. It presumably builds
in "value" conflicts and provides representation for the
lower orders.

Reanalysis of data from the study of Bennington,
Vermont, which I conducted with Robert D. Leigh and
Martin A. Trow, makes me very suspicious of this assumption. First, the mobility rate among leaders was only
half that among nonleaders, i.e., most political leaders
were high stationaries to begin with. Second, all of the
mobility among the leadership was upward. But, third
and most important, I think it is dangerous to assume
that upward social mobility necessarily provides political representation for the class left behind. Among the
upwardly mobile leaders in Bennington, I could find
little evidence of representation of the "masses." There
was rather more evidence of an exaggeration of the positions taken by the largest number of high stationary
political leaders, i.e., the "organization man" syndrome
examined by William F. Whyte.

There is yet a third way in which the pluralists
have tended to ignore or diminish the political significance of social class. Their focus on voting behavior
and political leadership is cast largely in terms of
individual motivation. To paraphrase Robert Dahl, "The
problem to explain is why anybody at all is highly active
in politics." I do not argue that an individualistic

psychological approach is entirely incorrect, but I do argue that it is incomplete and therefore inaccurate when it omits social class. For example, one of the pluralists has argued that if A collects blondes, B collects Renoirs and C collects politicians, the problem is to understand why C is so public-service oriented. But that is not the whole of the problem. If C does collect politicians, he may also collect tax exemptions. We must ask to whose benefit such tax exemptions redound: Only to C himself? Or to A and B as well, since all come from a class of actors with important political resources (money and status) which can be used by one for the benefit of all.

As a final comment on this topic, let me refer to an article on "Sources of Local Political Involvement" which appeared in the December 1968, *American Political Science Review*. In this article, Robert Alford and I reported that in examining those with high political involvement in local affairs, three characteristics--education, home-ownership, and organizational activity--had permitted the accurate classification of a full 85 percent of those in the highest involvement category. This indicates that such key social characteristics cannot be ignored if we are to develop a viable and useful political science.

THE UTILITY OF POLITICAL ACTION

My eighth point is that the pluralistic literature has ignored social class in yet another way, for it has failed to ask who benefits from the way the costs and burdens of public policy are allocated. Such failure leaves the reader believing that tax burdens of community policies are evenly and fairly spread--something that has been impossible to achieve at the national level of government, even with the progressive personal income tax. Each year, at income tax time, one finds the predictable spate of articles about individuals with earned incomes of a million dollars or more who nonetheless legally avoided paying even one penny of federal income tax. Are we to assume that state and local taxation is better than this?[7]

AN ECOLOGY OF POWER DISTRIBUTIONS

Ninth, the pluralistic literature also continues to ignore a suggestion offered as long ago as 1964 by Theodore Lowi (in his *World Affairs* review article on Bauer, Pool and Dexter's *American Business and Public Policy*). This is the possibility that there may be at least three different types of domestic policy, and that each is characterized by a distinctive distribution of power. In the area characterized as Distribution, one finds mutual noninterference and logrolling of the sort Kaufman and Sayre discovered in their *Governing New York City*. For Regulation, one finds interest group combat and coalitions of the sort Truman described in *The Governmental Process*. And, as reported by others, the "regulators" are typically captured by the "regulatees." Finally, for Redistribution, one finds an embattled but usually victorious elitist distribution of power such as that in Hunter's *Community Power Structure*.

If Lowi's suggestions prove useful in further research, then sociologists and political scientists cannot continue to assume that there is a single distribution of power characteristic of the community, for the latter should then be considered as an ecology of power distributions. Furthermore, it may be desirable to use the multiple-arenas-and-power-structures approach which Lowi advocates in the concluding chapter of *At the Pleasure of the Mayor*. Thus, one might reconcile Dahl and Hunter, each being correct within a limited focus. Most of the policies and decisions Hunter commented upon were in the areas of economic development and social welfare, where we would expect wealth and status to be prime sources of power. These are also areas in which we might expect to find an elite anxious to prevent any redistribution of power. Conversely, the issues with which Dahl deals--urban renewal and public education--seem to fit primarily into the distribution category.

MICROANALYSIS AND MACROANALYSIS

My final point, to which I have already alluded, is that Dahl's orientation to the individual nourishes microanalysis at the expense of macroanalysis. The gap is evident in the neglect of interest groups, of the "climate of effective opinion," and of political culture and elite subculture. It is evident also in the lack of attention to the private context of public affairs. This is merely hinted at in *Who Governs?*, where Dahl notes in passing that whatever urban renewal policies Mayor Richard Lee adopted had to be accomplished without a major increase in local taxes. That is, the private sphere places greater or lesser constraints on the public decisionmaking that can take place.

Similarly, in the study Robert Alford and I are conducting in Wisconsin, public decisionmaking in Kenosha seems utterly dependent on the level of operation of the Rambler American Motors plant there. This, in turn, is dependent upon decisions made by the "Big Three" in Detroit and by the federal government in Washington. The scope of public policymaking is certainly much more constrained there than in a city like Madison, whose economy is quite different. But this public/private relationship does not emerge clearly until one undertakes truly comparative field work, something the most prominent pluralists have not done.

THE QUALITY OF COMMUNITY POLITICS

Finally, in his concept of "indirect influence," Dahl asks us to believe of the local voter what the Survey Research Center and V.O. Key, Jr. in his *Public Opinion and American Democracy* failed to establish concerning the national voter--that (a) he knows who "his" incumbents are; (b) that he knows what their public record, e.g., roll call vote is; and (c) he cares, i.e., that he knows his own position and feels he can and should accomplish something by retaliatory voting. In

view of what I have already said, it should be obvious
that this model--with its emphasis on individualism,
rationality, visibility, responsibility and account-
ability--strains my credulity.

Yet this shortcoming fails to inhibit the pluralist
from making value judgments about the "stable" and
"viable" quality of "his" community. "His" community may
be stable indeed: perhaps this is why since 1964 New
Haven Negroes have resorted to unconventional political
strategies and tactics, up to and including violence and
destruction of property.

Whether such a community is viable is more open to
question. There are powerless groups in this society;
they are becoming more aware of their powerless condition
and more determined to do something about it. Whether we
are to have peaceful change, and thus a viable political
system, depends on whether we have an enlightened elite
that can acquiesce in the sharing of power. Yet it is
this elite which the pluralists maintain does not exist.

NOTES

Author's note: I am indebted to two of my colleagues at UCLA--John C. Ries and Richard M. Merelman--for their careful reading of an earlier version of this article. That it is not better is not their fault.

[1] Richard Merelman suggests that on the contrary the book is read, but with too much reverence. We agree, however, on my main point--the uncritical acceptance of the work.

[2] I do not wish to be misunderstood here. As Merelman has reminded me, Dahl's writings have the virtue of a certain tentativeness and an undogmatic quality.

[3] If the reader, like my colleague Merelman, should wonder how we can map "nondecisions," my answer is that the procedure will emerge only through comparative analysis. That is, when we take a sample of communities and observe that decision "X" arises in Community A, but not in Community B, then we can begin working backward to the suppression or elevation processes of the two polities.

[4] See my article, "The McCone Commission and Social Science," in *Phylon*, Summer 1968.

[5] I am not fully satisfied with my formulation of the problem, which may be oversimplified. However, Professor Robert R. Alford, of the Department of Sociology, University of Wisconsin, and I have data from our Wisconsin "Four Cities" study to test this proposition at least in primitive form.

[6] Alternatively, we might argue that even the best example of interest group pluralism, David Truman's *The Governmental Process*, fails to grasp the political importance of "social status" due to its anti-Brady, anti-Marxist stance. Truman's work merely diminishes the significance of social status in a manner to be discussed below.

[7]This failure has been noted by William C. Mitchell. But since it appeared in a place--his textbook on *The American Polity*--not likely to be read by too many political scientists, I repeat it here.

The Power Grid of the Metropolis

by G. ROSS STEPHENS

University of Missouri, Kansas City

CONTENTS

TABLES

SUMMARY

The elitist-pluralist controversy has now become a somewhat sterile academic exercise, for we are now in a comparative phase of community power studies. Claire Gilbert, for example, comparing 167 case studies of community power, concluded that small towns and cities are dominated by formally elected officials, but major decisions are postponed indefinitely. Middle-sized cities are ruled by nonpolitical persons or by a coalition of such individuals and elected officials, while large cities are led by elected officials who command whatever power there is.

What we perceive depends both upon what methods we use and where we look. Many studies focused on small towns, isolated cities, a few central cities and a suburb or two. This paper suggests that to gain a new perspective, we ought to look more intensively at the metropolitan area as a whole, in particular at the suburban elements as they relate to the entire urban complex. When consideration shifts from individual units to great cities and metropolitan areas, the power grid becomes much more complex. Further, while it can be argued that the metropolitan area as defined by the Census Bureau is not a community, it is, nevertheless, a spatial reality and the place where a large part of the population resides.

At present most of us, like other social scientists, are guilty of too much hypothesizing based on inadequate documentation. This seems to be particularly true of community power structure research. The recent trend towards comparative studies of community leadership has led to some improvement, but we still have little systematic and comparable research available, especially when we focus on the medium-to-large metropolitan complex that includes hundreds of political jurisdictions. We still know very little about the complicated web of relationships among elected officials, interest groups and residents of the areas being served, or about the character

of the individual jurisdictions. If such political variables are important to policy outcomes, then we need to
know a great deal more about the power grid of the
metropolis; and we need far more systematic and comparable political data on local governing areas.

Unfortunately, collection of such data is extremely
expensive and far beyond the capability of the average
researcher. In addition, it would take a massive effort
to collect and standardize existing political information. As you know, one problem with existing census
tract information is that the tracts often do not parallel political boundaries. For research purposes it is
imperative to rectify this lack of conformity. Several
persons have suggested creating political census tracts
conforming to the political subdivisions of the metropolis. Such an undertaking would be highly desirable if
some agreement could be reached on the data to be collected. But the possibility of obtaining this type of
information is lessened by the need to obtain congres-
sional approval. Some items might, however, gradually
be bootlegged. In fact, a few such items have been
included in the present research.

DIMENSIONS OF COMMUNITY POWER

The Structure of Formal Government

It is assumed that community power includes political power as well as the role of government. It is
admittedly difficult to separate the "political" from the
"social," and governmental from non-governmental group
action. Yet we agree that the structure of formal
government has some relationship to the power structure
of the community as a whole, and that attention must be
paid to the geographic reach of those who participate in
the decision process. One conclusion seems certain, however. At present, metropolitan area government fragmentation means that the power and influence of officials
and other actors is equally fragmented. Thus, in most
metropolitan areas there is neither an areawide

governmental agency with general powers, nor a metropolitan constituency. Limited discretion and limited action
often result in stalemate. "Too many cooks not only
spoil the stew--they may prevent its ever being assembled
in the pot."[1] That is, in our system of very limited
local government, negative power is far more prevalent
than positive power, and power itself may become so diffuse that it almost disappears.

The Bases of Political Power

The bases of power in the metropolis are multiple.
So much has been said and written about the role of the
economic elite that it is almost redundant to say that
money is power. But so are votes and group support that
at times may be translated into votes. Political office
in the metropolitan area conforms to legal boundaries,
which establish spatial limits to power, and it is a rare
public official who can claim a metropolitan constituency as his own. Unless there is an atypically effective political party organization, the influence of parties and of elected officials does not appreciably tran-
scend boundaries. Further, such misguided reforms as the
direct primary and nonpartisan elections have tended to
weaken local party organizations.

At the same time, local governments are becoming
more bureaucratized and more professional. As they
become more professional, the administrative bureaucracies are also becoming more independent in the core city
as well as in the larger suburban and county governments.
Special districts and authorities are especially notori-
ous examples of such independence. More and more,
bureaucracy is a factor to be reckoned with as a source
of power, one that changes the character of local government.

The professional bureaucrat at the local level may
be more responsive to the wishes and demands of professional bureaucrats at the state or national levels than

to locally elected political leaders. This characteristic of "vertical functional autocracy" is a concomitant of the professionalization of bureaucracy. Wallace Sayre and Herbert Kaufman have described the mayor of New York City as a mediator among contending interests and great public bureaucracies: he has no real power to control the government over which he presides.[2] The city is at best a polyarchy. New York may be an extreme case, but there is reason to believe that similar tendencies exist in all governments large enough to support a professional bureaucracy.

Contemporary urban society faces the possibility of major conflict between Blacks and whites, rich and poor, labor unions and great public bureaucracies. Negro communities are developing into important bases of group support and group conflict. In some places where riots have occurred, the predominantly white police bureaucracies have been responsible to no one but themselves, thus stimulating proposals for the establishment of police review boards with citizen representation.

In some instances, while religious or social position may form a kind of power base, so too may special knowledge or skill. The introduction of computer technology adds a new dimension to the power matrix. This is obvious from what has happened in business and industry, universities and public bureaucracies: it takes a large organization to utilize current technology effectively. Moreover, not everyone can talk to the computer and utilize its output. Thus control of computer input and output becomes a source of power in a technical-bureaucratic society. Further, the economics of computer technology favors the large centralized installation.

In summary, there are varying degrees of independence and interdependence among the contending power structures. "Fat cats" exercise influence beyond their numerical strength; money can be used to influence elections; some groups do receive special treatment. Overall, public and private bureaucracies and their allied interests are more important today than in the past. And

the ability to utilize knowledge and modern technology is
a factor that cannot be ignored.

Issue Areas and Political Participation

Another dimension of the power grid of the metropolis is the policy issue and/or governmental function(s)
involved in the decision process, and the group to which
the issue appeals. Taxation, land development, political participation, race and the host of functional issues
(such as education, transportation, housing and urban
renewal, health and welfare) elicit the participation of
different constellations of groups, business organizations, governments and bureaucracies. For example, the
groups that are effective in a Community Chest campaign
drive may be unable to muster support for a bond issue
for public education or mass transit. Groups and officials with important influence on the consolidation or
reorganization of public health activities may have
little or no influence on the control of air pollution.

The Spatial Aspect of Power

Finally, the geographic dimension must be
considered--the physical or spatial area through which
leadership, influence or control can be exercised. Some
sectors, like finance, may be far more influential in the
core city and the higher income suburbs than in industrial suburbs. Labor's influence is prominent in the
core city and in working class and industrial suburbs,
while Black political power appears limited largely to
the core city. Similarly, such groups play different
roles at the state and national level. In any event, the
size and complexity of the metropolitan community is an
important determinant of the nature of community power.
The constellation of groups at the local level may not be
too different from one metropolitan area to the next, but
their effectiveness and power could vary considerably.

In summary, community power structure in the metropolis has at least four dimensions: the power base(s); the multiple governmental jurisdictions; the kinds of policy decision(s) under scrutiny; and the region through which influence is or can be exercised. There are, of course, many intervening and exogenous variables, not the least of which are the activities of state and national governments.

METROPOLITAN LEADERSHIP

In considering community power structure, too little emphasis has been given to the elected officials of the municipal baronies that comprise the metropolis, i.e., municipal mayors and councilmen as well as trustees of suburban towns and townships. Considerable effort has been directed toward the study of small town leadership; toward determining the economic elite in communities of various sizes; toward eliciting the attitudes of residents, mayors and managers; and toward describing ways in which particular issues are decided. But very little is known about suburban elected officials, their role and involvement in the local political process, and their relationship to the attributes of the residents and community itself.

Studies of local political leadership have usually emphasized the informal leadership, at times neglecting elected municipal representatives. Perhaps the latter are assumed to be unimportant; perhaps the resources needed are not available to the average researcher; or possibly both explanations are applicable. Admittedly, the municipality is not governed in a vacuum: in every community there are important and influential persons who do not hold public office. But we have tended to look for these individuals and groups at the expense of the elected representatives. By virtue of holding office, the latter have a role in local politics though it may be limited by external factors and sometimes may be more negative than positive.

This "public official" approach assumes that elected officials are not necessarily the servants of the economic elite. Instead, it assumes that there is a "power structure" in every organized activity, and that there are many relationships possible among the power sectors in society. Further, within each sector, there is usually the dominance of a minority. Specifically, within the scope of their limited powers, political officials are usually more influential than are the economic elite in their sector.

The issue may, in some instances, focus on the limitation of the powers of public officials. Why are they so limited? Too many municipalities in fact are little more than "fund managers and bookkeeping operations."[3]

In every community and metropolitan area there are groups and individuals who have a stake in the nonexistence of an effective decision-making structure. That is, they have a stake in the maintenance of the status quo of limited and impotent local government in core cities, fragmented and easily influenced policies for suburban governments and the manager-governed "nonpolitical" policies of medium-sized towns.

Land development, rapidly assuming critical importance in most urban areas, exemplifies the kind of issue that involves important interests. If urban government should deal effectively with questions of development, the results would threaten realtors, land speculators and bankers. Clearly, private decisions, no matter how numerous in the aggregate, do not add up to a public policy. Similarly, the many public decisions reached by the fragmented governments of the metropolitan region do not create a viable public policy for the area as a whole.

Despite their limitations, local officials do provide channels of communications to larger governments; they are effective as an interest group; and they constitute a vital component of our mythology of self-government. They do make limited decisions, some of which are vital to an understanding of the system. For instance they control services and activities that have a direct impact upon the life-style of the community, e.g., public schools, zoning and subdivision regulations, housing and local police protection.

COMMUNITY ATTRIBUTES AND COMMUNITY SERVICES

Williams and others, in noting that the variation in municipal policies is related to the social and political ecology of the metropolis, have pointed out the need to consider the spatially defined domicile or place of residence as identifying the basic political unit.[4] Williams has also established a continuum showing that certain local services (e.g., public schools and zoning policies) are necessary to maintain the life-style of the suburban community, while other activities, designated as system-maintaining, are necessary for the integration and functioning of the metropolis as a whole (e.g., communications and major highways). Table I represents this continuum.

The "life-style maintaining" services are probably fairly similar--in incidence but not quality--from one locale to another. Certain system maintaining services are more apt to show variation. Where the supply of water is critical, centralization of water services might well be placed high on the list of system maintaining activities. Other services vary up and down the continuum, according to the situation in the individual metropolitan area. A few services will, of course, be neutral.

In order to understand fully the politics of the metropolis, it is necessary to relate the attributes of the local governing area to the characteristics of locally elected officials, and the attributes of their governments to policy stands on local, intermunicipal and metropolitan issues. At present our lack of knowledge about the politics of the metropolis, more specifically the politics of suburbia, extends not only to the policy

TABLE I

CONTINUUM OF COMMUNITY SERVICES

Life-style maintaining services:	Neutral services:	System maintaining services:
Public schools Zoning and housing policy Local police protection		Communications Major highways

issues that elicit consensus and conflict, but also to the characteristics of individuals elected to local public office. We have folklore about local representatives and issues, but relatively little hard data.

The Williams continuum could be useful in developing hypotheses about suburban policies. We might postulate, for example, that the type of individual recruited to local public office depends, at least in part, on the functional specialization of the suburban community. To do this, we need a typology of local governing areas that includes such attributes as urban and nonurban patterns, land use, economic character and social attributes of the residents.

SUMMARY: TYPOLOGY OF LOCAL AREAS

A. Rural-urban continuum

1. Rural: places of less than 20,000 inhabitants outside metropolitan and submetropolitan areas
   a. Village: fewer than 1,000 inhabitants
   b. Town: more than 1,000 inhabitants but fewer than 20,000

2. Submetropolitan: from 20,000 to 50,000 inhabitants

3. Metropolitan: classed as a Standard Metropolitan Statistical Area (SMSA) by the U.S. Census Bureau, with 50,000 or more inhabitants in the core city or cities
   a. Fringe
   b. Suburban
   c. Core

4. Great cities and their metropolitan regions: SMSAs 2,000,000 plus
   a. Fringe
   b. Suburban
   c. Core

B. Economic character[a]

1. Extractive, e.g., logging, mining
2. Agricultural, e.g., farming, ranching
3. Residential

        4. Industrial
        5. Commercial
        6. Balanced
        7. Specialized, e.g., resort, university, govern-
           ment

   C. Social character of the population
        1. Social rank (occupation, education and income)
        2. Ethnic composition of the community
        3. Life-style (fertility ratios, women in the labor
           force, types of dwelling units)

   D. Political character
        1. Partisan or nonpartisan elections
        2. Past partisan behavior, e.g., voting patterns
        3. Election method, e.g., by ward or at-large, size
           of district
        4. Competition for office
        5. Governmental structure, e.g., mayor-council,
           commission, council-manager

   ─────────
   [a]Nonexclusive types.

Some work on community attributes has already been
done. Eyestone and Eulau used self-administered questionnaires to study local policy outcomes relative to
community development.[6] Henry Schmandt, in a small study
of city councils in the Milwaukee area, found that the
type of individual recruited to city council positions is
partly a function of the kind of suburban community
involved: industrial communities had more blue-collar
workers, and bedroom communities had more professionals
and managers as councilmen.[7] Charles Adrian suggests
that the average city councilman is a local businessman
active in community organizations, frequently a college
graduate, i.e., a typical middle-class merchant or manager.[8] A quick look in Table II at the data for 10
municipalities in the Kansas City metropolitan area cor-
roborates the findings of Schmandt in Milwaukee. While
other studies could be cited, these are sufficient to
show that some of the results are inconclusive, and to
suggest that many of the studies do not have the depth
necessary for an investigation of the political ecology
of the metropolis.

If we are to link political structures, elected
officials and policy outcomes to something like the
Williams continuum, data about political characteristics
of the individual municipalities must be included in our
typology. Partisanship or the lack of it in local elections; voting patterns; election structure (district or
at-large); size of voting district; amount of competition for office; and the size and type of the local
governments are all relevant. In the Kansas City area,
for example, there are some 137 municipalities and townships, and nearly 700 elected municipal and township
officials. If we count all locally elected public officials, there are more than twice this number; by 1970
the figure will increase to about 1,750. Yet this is
only a medium size metropolitan complex.

A survey of all locally elected officials in even
one metropolitan area would be a major undertaking. In
the nation's Standard Metropolitan Statistical Areas,

TABLE II

OCCUPATIONAL CLASSIFICATION OF 101 MAYORS AND CITY COUNCILMEN IN 10 MUNICIPALITIES BY TYPE OF GOVERNING AREA, CITY AND SUBURB, 1968

	Central city	Suburbs				
		High income residential	Middle income residential[a]	Older balanced	Industrial	Overall average
Professional and technical	62%	44%	20%	14%	- %	25%
Other white collar	23	44	72	59	43	56
Service and blue collar	-	-	-	27	57	12
Housewife or retired	15	12	8	-	-	7

[a]One suburb has two governing bodies performing municipal activities--a city council and a lake association. Both are included without materially affecting the distribution.

there are 75,600 municipal and township officers elected out of a total of 133,800.[9] If we should ever develop a political census tract, we should certainly survey the characteristics of the half million of us who occupy local elective positions. But an undertaking of this magnitude is clearly beyond the capability of the individual researcher, unless he resorts to sampling.

If the life-style maintaining activities of the community are, in fact, controlled by individual political leaders, intensive research along these lines is needed to understand policy outcomes within the urban complex. We might ask if the toy governments of suburbia are able to deal effectively with issues affecting the life-styles of their jurisdictions, or whether they are caught up in the larger forces at work in our society. Similarly, system maintaining activities must function at some minimum level of efficiency if chaos is to be avoided. Yet the present ad hoc arrangements for administering these activities--privately owned utilities, informal or haphazard regulation and coordination by larger governments, occasional single-function special authorities--may not suffice as increased demands are put upon the system.

At present, the number of system maintaining activities is on the increase. The need for all kinds of pollution control is one example. Another is the possible need to establish a truly integrated transportation system. Past overemphasis on airplane and automobile transport, with no attempt at integration, has left a sorry legacy. Witness the problems of the airlines as newer and larger machines are introduced, or the rape of our cities through use of the private auto as the sole means of internal transport. Theoretically, solutions might be attained at the metropolitan level if there were a metropolitan government with the resources and ability to act. But technology has outstripped our political system: we have the technological, economic and organizational ability to restructure our cities, but seem politically incapable of action.

LARGER GOVERNMENTS

To assume a community power structure is to assume a structure with the ability, resources and authority to deal with community problems. This is rarely the case in the nation's metropolitan areas. National and state governments are building administrative decision structures with major effects on the urban complex. The national government has large administrative bureaucracies with the potential for controlling the really important decisions that affect our urban areas, i.e., DOT (Department of Transportation), HEW (Department of Health, Education, and Welfare), HUD (Department of Housing and Urban Development) and DOD (Department of Defense). Many states have or plan to establish little HUDs and DOTs, among them Connecticut, New Jersey and New York. With nationwide and statewide decision mechanisms for transportation, urban affairs, health and welfare, combined with the private decision-making machinery of the corporation, there may be little left for the individual community to decide other than the color of the local airline terminal building.

Consider what is happening in transportation. In its long-range planning, the Department of Transportation looks ahead to nationally integrated transportation. It would be logical for some of this integration to occur within the metropolis, but no local integrating agency exists. Airline traffic, for example, is slowing down as a result of congestion at major terminals. And with the advent of the jumbo jet, the problem of getting passengers to and from the terminal in private automobiles will be virtually insoluble. Similarly, we have neglected mass transit to our own detriment. Further, nearly every new expressway in the country is opposed by the people affected by the routes chosen. It appears that a truly integrated transportation system will have to come from above: it will not be achieved voluntarily, or through the actions of many local units. Some, in fact, are predicting that the present system will grind to a halt long before such an integrated network can be achieved.

CONCLUSION

The power grid of the metropolis, as it currently exists, has many dimensions. However, we know little about the way the current system operates, about its political ecology, and about the impact of state and national policies. Theoretically, it is possible that such knowledge might soon become irrelevant, that the power grid would be fundamentally altered by state and national governments exercising their full potential influence. Practically, such a massive shift is unlikely, due to the extensive diversion of resources it would require. Thus real knowledge about the way our metropolitan areas are governed is not an antiquarian pursuit. But it will take considerably more research effort than we have put forth to date.

NOTES

[1] Scott Greer, "The Shaky Future of Local Government,"
Psychology Today, 2(3): 64-69 (1968). See especially
p. 64.

[2] See their *Governing New York City* (New York: Norton,
1965).

[3] This phrase is attributed to Matthew Holden, Wayne
State University.

[4] Oliver P. Williams, "Life Style Values and Political
Decentralization in Metropolitan Areas," *Southwestern
Social Science Quarterly*, 48(3): 299-310 (1967); and
Williams, Harold Herman, Charles S. Liebman and Thomas R.
Dye, *Suburban Differences and Metropolitan Policies*
(Philadelphia: University of Pennsylvania Press, 1965).

[5] This typology is an adaption of one used in a recent
research project by the author, and is outlined in
Table I. See G. Ross Stephens, "Mediopolis: A Simple
Fiscal Model of the Metropolis" (Kansas City: Institute
of Community Studies, May 1968), preliminary draft.

[6] Robert Eyestone and Heinz Eulau, "City Councils and
Policy Outcomes: A Study of Development in a Metropoli-
tan Region." Paper at the annual meeting of the American
Political Science Association, 1966.

[7] Henry J. Schmandt, "The City and the Ring," *American
Behavioral Scientist*, 4(3): 17-19 (1960).

[8] Charles R. Adrian and Charles Press, *Governing Urban
America* (New York: McGraw-Hill, 1968), pp. 244-250.

[9] See "Popularly Elected Officials of State and Local
Governments," U.S. Bureau of the Census, *Census of
Governments, 1967*, 6(1): 1-5, 45-46, 53 (Washington,
D.C.: 1968).

Why Study Power Structures?
A Critique and A Theoretical Proposal

by JOHN WALTON
Northwestern University

CONTENTS

FIGURE

Community power structure studies are old enough, and voluminous enough, to have reached the age of accountability. It might be impetuous to ask a younger and less actively practiced specialty how far it had progressed toward fulfilling its initial promise. However, as the study of community power nears the end of its second decade, boasting over 300 titles specifically concerned with the topic, the time for a critical appraisal of what has been accomplished seems to be at hand.[1]

Presumably the reason for analyzing the distribution and exercise of power in any social organization, e.g., factory, community or nation, is that such knowledge will provide clues about its operation, interaction and change processes. Power analysis, like any conceptual orientation, must be justified by what it explains, not by the intriguing imagery it evokes.[2] Judged by these criteria, the initial promise of community power studies has yet to be fulfilled.

This is clear if we examine the current status of the field. First, it is excessively descriptive. Moreover, this descriptive emphasis is concerned chiefly with only one of many potentially interesting problems, i.e., how broadly or narrowly power is distributed. Second, students of community power are preoccupied with technique at the expense of substance. Although the fading controversy between reputational and decisional methods was partly, perhaps excessively, an issue focused on technique, the research results at least provided substantive information to the reader with more general interests. Recent methodological "breakthroughs" have been accomplished through gross simplifications of the power process and at the expense of any understanding of its dynamics. The principle seems to be the study of the maximum number of localities with the maximum degree of superficiality.

Third, while recent studies have begun to formulate and test propositions, they tend to be trivial and are generated from common sense rather than explicit theoretical statements. But if the propositions tested are not deductive, neither are they inductive. In fact, the literature contains few attempts to generate more general testable relationships from a limited set of simple and apparently valid propositions.[3]

It should be understood that this appraisal is not a criticism of description, technique and simple propositions. All are necessary aspects of the research process. However, these activities have been emphasized at the expense of formulating and evaluating more general explanations in methodologically appropriate ways. In short, the field continues to be atheoretical.

The atheoretical status of the field is clarified if we first conceive of power as either a dependent or an independent variable. We then can ask what we know of the causes or concomitants of various types of power arrangement.[4] A few studies have addressed this question, usually at a rather low level of generalization. Efforts have been made to link the size, economic structure and social characteristics of the community to the type of power structure. Unfortunately, such studies fail to explain why a given social or economic condition should be associated with a certain type of power arrangment. On closer examination, these studies assume that as towns become larger and more complex, their power structures become more competitive. The statement is trivial, perhaps even untrue. What we need are more specific propositions drawn from the body of social organization theory, rather than being pulled from the hat of common sense.

The utility of power as an independent variable raises similar questions. For example, how does the distribution of power in a social organization affect performance and change in that organization? Power structure studies have produced little hard data[5] and few

theoretical ideas on this topic.[6] We do not even know
what types of power arrangements promote urban development or decay, much less why they are related. When confronted with such questions, students of community power
structure must remain silent. At most, they may offer
some platitude about the virtues of democracy in promoting change, a relationship the literature itself does not
support.

In summary, students of community power have assumed
that their subject is indeed important in understanding
the character of community life, as well as the direction
of social change. Yet little has been done to lend substance to the assumption. If this criticism is to be
overcome, future research and theorizing must place
greater emphasis on developing and testing general propositions.

A profitable beginning might be made by recognizing
that the community is a social organization. It is fer-
tile ground for testing a variety of ideas developed in
closely related areas, such as studies of labor unions,
factories, political parties, prisons and hospitals.
This extension of theoretical perspectives should be
accompanied by more specific, theoretically based studies
of the causes and consequences of power in social organizations. We might ask how increasing size and specialization of an organization affect the distribution of
power. (No one, for example, has yet asked if Michels
has any relevance to communities.) Or we might ask what
kinds of power arrangements are conducive to solving
urban problems. The following research outline illus-
trates the type of approach suggested.

POWER AND ECONOMIC DEVELOPMENT

Economic development is an appropriate area for
applying such an approach, for the economic development
of a locality discloses a great deal about its social
organization. Students of community decisionmaking would

probably assume that the organization of power is a critical variable in explaining the level and distribution of
material resources, i.e., economic development. Their
assumption is shared by a number of theorists who concern
themselves with the noneconomic causes of economic
growth.

Although space does not permit complete documentation of the importance often attached to power and decisionmaking, a few quotations will illustrate the point.
Hoselitz argues that:

> ...since there seems to exist a con-
> siderable body of empirical evidence
> that in presently underdeveloped
> countries economic leadership is
> concentrated among a group of people
> who also control political power, a
> reallocation of patterns of respon-
> sibility and authority demands a
> shift of political power from the
> present political elite to a dif-
> ferent one and the simultaneous
> reshuffling of the status system
> of the society.[7]

Similarly, Horowitz is critical of certain conventional approaches to development because they are insen-
sitive to those structural features of underdeveloped
societies that are responsible for the societies' economic condition:

> The chief fact to be recognized is
> that very few of the "have" sectors
> of a society are willing to pay the
> full price of rapid economic pro-
> gress....where economic and political
> power is concentrated in the hands of
> a small group, whose main interest is
> in the preservation of the status quo,
> prospects for economic progress are

> very slight unless a social revolu-
> tion effects a shift in the distri-
> bution of income and power.[8]

From a different vantage point Hirschmann calls
attention to the capacity for decisionmaking:

> Our diagnosis is simply that countries
> fail to take advantage of their devel-
> opment potential because, for reasons
> largely related to their image of
> change, they find it difficult to take
> the decisions needed for development
> in the required number and with the
> required speed...the shortages in
> specific factors or "prerequisites"
> of production are interpreted as a
> manifestation of the basic defi-
> ciency in organization.... We have
> identified the ability to make such
> decisions as the scarce resource
> which conditions all other scarcities
> and difficulties in underdeveloped
> countries.[9]

This agreement on the importance of power and decisionmaking reflects the faith that has long animated
enthusiasts of community power analysis. Thus it raises
the question noted above: Can we understand the change
represented by economic development through an analysis
of power relations? While a number of theorists affirm
this point of view, little research has been done on the
precise nature of the relationship between power arrangements and economic change. Yet, given a systematic theoretical statement, extension of the power structure
research tradition to the field of economic development
should be both possible and productive.

Specifically, a marriage of specialities--the application of power structure research methods to the study
of economic development--has two advantages. First, it

provides a relatively rigorous methodological basis for analyzing the role of power in development. Second, it provides a way out of the narrowness and theoretical irrelevance of current power structure research. In short, it opens the field to those larger theoretical issues of social organization and change that are the most productive alternatives for future research.

THEORETICAL ORIENTATION

The following remarks present a small scale illustration of the form a theoretical statement about power and change might take. In an abbreviated fashion it sets out certain definitions; elaborates these by reference to assumptions drawn from the field of social organization; and derives from them several general propositions. Space precludes thorough exploration of the assumptions and propositions that the model suggests, as do the limited purposes of this paper.

Concepts

1. *Power* is the capacity to mobilize resources for the accomplishment of intended effects with recourse to some type of sanction(s) to encourage compliance. *Capacity* distinguishes power from "right" or *authority*; recourse to sanctions distinguishes power from *influence*, which involves only the ability to mobilize resources. The notion of capacity also suggests that power need not be exercised overtly, but may be included in potential or latent ability.[10] Moreover, power does not depend on success in accomplishing intended effects; one may lose a contest and still be said to have power. Finally, the definition implies intention, distinguishing power from unintentional control.[11]

2. For present purposes, a social organization may be thought of as a system that sets limits on the behavior of actors by (a) assigning them functions in a

process of allocation and (b) relating these functions in a process of integration.[12]

    3. Accordingly:

> Organization may be seen not only as
> structural conditions (or positions)
> and functional necessities (or work
> to be accomplished) but also as a
> continuous process wherein the needs
> of a given society are met through
> cooperative systems. Such systems
> are not fixed immutably; they change
> as the nature of the environment
> changes.[13]

    4. In order to accomplish certain ends, power is differentially invested in organizational functions. All organizations are characterized by an unequal distribution of power, although the extent of inequality varies.

Assumptions

    5. The total amount of power available to actors in a social organization at a given time may increase or decrease.[14]

    6. In any social organization, no actors are totally powerful or totally powerless, for the persistence of the organization requires some minimal level of cooperation, which must always be bought at a price.[15]

    7. The wide distribution of power suggests that stable power arrangements are, in a broad sense, negotiated arrangements. Suitable incentives for cooperation must be worked out, although the negotiation process may be tacit and the agenda of negotiable items minimal.[16] To emphasize this "exchange" or "interchange" model, we shall subsequently refer to the context in which decisions are reached as the "negotiation process."

"Decision-making process" may occasionally be substituted, provided this too is understood in a broad sense.

8. By virtue of the allocation of functions and the differential investment of power in these functions, all social organizations embody divergent ideologies (in the Mannheimian sense, i.e., limited perspectives rooted in social organizational positions). The negotiation process is conditioned by the nature of these ideologies, as well as by the extent of their divergence and conflict.

9. Arrangements of power are inherently unstable. The exercise of power may increase an actor's total power. Similarly--and perhaps more typically--one's total power may be decreased by the accumulated compromises into which one enters. The persistence of a given power arrangement depends on the stability, flexibility and renewability of its capacity to mobilize resources.[17]

Propositions

In our analysis, "directed change" is the central dependent variable. Directed change may be defined as intentional change that extends cooperative activity and increases participation in the benefits of the social organization.

The two basic principles of social organization are useful for deriving a set of power arrangements that can then be related to directed change. *Integration of functions* refers to the organization or cohesiveness of power; *allocation of functions* refers to the distribution of power. Combining the two dimensions we obtain the typology of power arrangements present in Figure I.

FIGURE I

TYPOLOGY OF POWER ARRANGEMENTS

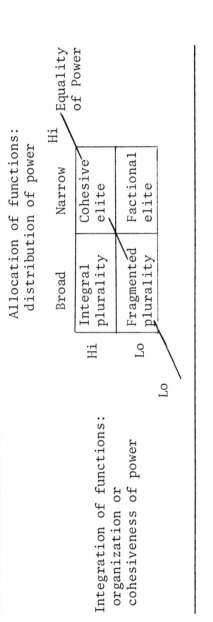

Figure I is reminiscent of others, especially those suggested by Agger, Goldrich and Swanson.[18] However, other typologies usually fail to deal empirically with the two-dimensionality of power distributions, i.e., they may be broad or narrow, flat (rectangular) or peaked. Substantively, power may be distributed among many actors or few, i.e., broadly or narrowly, and these actors may be more or less equally powerful. For example, the electoral college system for selecting U.S. Presidents is a broad but unequal power arrangement, because the California voter has more impact on the outcome than does his neighbor in Nevada. A direct popular vote would be a broad, equal power arrangement.

Because the quality of power has important implications for its exercise, it can be added to the two variables in the typology, producing eight possible power arrangements. Figure I shows the variable operating on two of the types. The relevance of the typology becomes clear as we consider a few of the more obvious propositions that flow from it.

10. The broader the distribution of power in an organization, the more extensive are the areas that must be negotiated in making concessions and securing cooperation. This situation makes directed change more likely.

11. Conversely, the broader the distribution of power in an organization, the more intensive, i.e., less tacit, is the negotiation process. Directed change is therefore more likely.

12. Conversely, the greater the equality of power, the more extensive the veto power. As this produces stalemates in the negotiation process, directed change is less likely. There is some optimal balance of power equality/inequality in which more powerful groups can act effectively while still being dependent on, and accountable to, less powerful elements.

13. The greater the integration of power within a broad constituency, the more likely is coordinated action. Thus directed change is more likely.

14. As divergent ideologies are increasingly represented in the negotiation process, the range of negotiable alternatives becomes broader. This too increases the likelihood of directed change.

15. To the extent that increases in the total amount of power in the system promote a broader distribution of power, a more integrated distribution of power, an effective balance in equality/inequality relations, and greater representation of divergent ideologies, directed change becomes more likely.

16. All of the factors mentioned above operate simultaneously and interact with one another. For example, the optimal balance of power equality/inequality varies with the extent of integration: as integration of functions increases, greater equality of power will not be inimical to directed change. Similar qualifications affect all possible combinations. *Basically, directed change requires that powerful groups be sufficiently dependent to offer concessions in the negotiation process, yet sufficiently integrated and autonomous to undertake effective action.*

DERIVED PROPOSITIONS: THE CASE OF POWER AND ECONOMIC DEVELOPMENT

Communities, urban areas and nations fall within our category of social organizations. Thus they can be analyzed using the above theoretical orientation. Similarly, economic development is one example of the directed change we have been discussing. Accordingly, we now have at our disposal the elements necessary for a theoretically based study of the role of power in social organizational change.

The propositions that follow apply specifically to the economically underdeveloped societies of the Third World, as well as to regions or communities within those societies. They rest on the assumption, particularly applicable to the Third World, that economic development is a salient goal of most members of society.

This does not imply "value integration" or "ideological consensus." Indeed, there may be substantial conflict over the means of achieving economic development, as well as over its value as a means or an end. However, it does imply that Third World nations are increasingly aware of their relative and absolute deprivation, and that this awareness has given birth to a variety of modernizing ideologies characterized by the desire for better material circumstances. (This assumption is believed to be true of the vast majority of Third World societies.) Where such goals do not prevail, the following propositions would not apply.

17. The broader the distribution of power among the actors involved in economic production, the greater the likelihood of directed change aimed at promoting economic development.

18. The greater the number and relative value of concessions offered in the negotiation process, the greater the likelihood of directed change aimed at promoting economic development. Such concessions might include social mobility and access to positions of greater power.

19. The greater the equality of power, the more difficult it will be to formulate and execute directed change aimed at promoting economic development.

20. The greater the integration of power among a broad constituency of actors involved in economic production, the greater the likelihood of directed change aimed at economic development.

21. The greater the representation of divergent ideologies in the negotiation process, the greater the

likelihood of directed change aimed at promoting economic development.

22. To the extent that changes in the total power available to actors involved in economic production result in a broader distribution of power, directed change aimed at promoting economic development becomes more likely. The same relationship holds when changes in the total power available to actors involved in economic production result in a more integrated distribution of power, an effective balance of equality/inequality, and greater representation of divergent ideologies.

The foregoing theoretical exercise is offered for illustrative and perhaps heuristic purposes. The school is highly abstract and would undoubtedly require modification and specification in the course of applying it empirically. Thus, it is not intended as a theory. Rather, it is an analytic paradigm that specifies the meaning, concomitants and consequences of power. There is, I believe, little justification for studies of power structure that fail to meet these specifications.

NOTES

Author's note: I am grateful to Charles M. Bonjean who carefully read an earlier draft of this paper and made many helpful comments.

[1] Roland J. Pellegrin, "Selected Bibliography on Community Power Structure," *Southwestern Social Sciences Quarterly*, 48(3): 451-465 (1967).

[2] Technically speaking, concepts do not explain: they are essential parts of theories, which do explain. Throughout this paper, the term "theory" will be used in what I take to be its correct sense, i.e., "A scientific theory is a deductive system in which observable consequences logically follow from the conjunction of observed facts with the set of the fundamental hypotheses of the system." R.B. Braithwaite, *Scientific Explanation* (New York: Harper Torchbooks, 1960), p. 22.

[3] The only clear example I know of such an attempt is my paper, "Differential Patterns of Community Power Structure: An Explanation Based on Interdependence" in Terry N. Clark, ed., *Community Structure and Decision-Making: Comparative Analyses* (San Francisco: Chandler Publishing Co., 1968), pp. 441-459.

[4] The best available discussion on this topic is a forthcoming paper by Michael Aiken of the University of Wisconsin, "The Distribution of Community Power: Structural Bases and Social Consequences."

[5] See Aiken, ibid; Amos Hawley, "Community Power Structure and Urban Renewal Success," *American Journal of Sociology*, 68(4): 422-431 (1963); Terry N. Clark, "Community Structure, Decision-Making, Budget Expenditures and Urban Renewal in 51 American Communities," *American Sociological Review*, 33(4): 576-593 (1968).

164

[6] The only clear example here is Edward C. Banfield, *Political Influence* (New York: The Free Press, 1961). See also Marilyn Gittell, "A Typology of Power for Measuring Social Change," *The American Behavioral Scientist*, 9(8): 23-28 (1966).

[7] Berthold F. Hoselitz, *Sociological Aspects of Economic Growth* (New York: The Free Press, 1960), p. 49.

[8] Quoted in Irving Louis Horowitz, *Three Worlds of Development: The Theory and Practice of International Stratification* (New York: Oxford University Press, 1966), p. 214.

[9] Albert O. Hirschman, *The Strategy of Economic Development* (New Haven: Yale University Press, 1958), pp. 25 and 27.

[10] A recent discussion of the rationale behind these conventions is Dennis Wrong's "Some Problems in Defining Social Power," *American Journal of Sociology*, 73(6): 673-681 (1968).

[11] Wrong, ibid.

[12] This formulation is drawn directly from Scott Greer, *Social Organization* (New York: Random House, 1955).

[13] Greer, ibid., p. 6.

[14] Robert S. Lynd, "Power in American Society as Resource and Problem," in Arthur Kornhauser, ed., *Problems of Power in American Democracy* (Detroit: Wayne State University Press, 1957), pp. 1-45.

[15] The best work on this point is Gresham M. Sykes, *Society of Captives: A Study of a Maximum Security Prison*, (New York: Atheneum Books, 1966), especially his Chapter 3, "The Defects of Total Power." Also see David Riesman, "Some Observations on the Limits of Totalitarian Power" in his *Individualism Reconsidered* (Glencoe, Ill.: The Free Press, 1954), Chapter 25.

[16] A study illustrative of this point is Anselm Strauss, "The Hospital as a Negotiated Order" in Eliot Freidson,

ed., *The Hospital in Modern Society* (New York: The Free Press, 1963), pp. 147-169.

[17]An excellent discussion of the consequences of modernization for social structure and power arrangements is Arthur L. Stinchcombe, "Social Structure and Organizations" in James G. March, ed., *Handbook of Organizations* (Chicago: Rand McNally, 1965), pp. 142-193.

[18]See Robert E. Agger, Daniel Goldrich and Bert E. Swanson, *The Rulers and the Ruled: Political Power and Impotence in American Communities* (New York: John Wiley and Sons, 1964), p. 73.

**An Exploratory Study of Decisionmaking
and Development in a Mexican City**
by JOHN WALTON

CONTENTS

TABLES

This case study is the first in a research project dealing with economic development in four areas of Latin America. The research was formulated in accordance with the considerations discussed in the preceding paper. I have chosen to present the two separately so as to reflect more accurately the history of the early stages of the project. As will become apparent, I did not develop a set of generalized notions and then go out in the field to find them confirmed (as the typical style of a research paper would suggest to the reader). Rather, the initial approach speculated on the consequences that various concepts of power organization might have for directed change and development. At first, field work was highly exploratory and, as I shall indicate, led to some important modifications of the approach. In order to show this process, I will present a brief report on the procedures and results of some work done in Guadalajara, Mexico.

RESEARCH METHODS

If the foregoing discussion suggested the utility of analyzing economic development from the standpoint of power structure and decisionmaking, the techniques worked out by sociologists and political scientists should seem particularly appropriate. Because this literature is extensive and well known, no thorough discussion of it is necessary here. Suffice it to say that the techniques have developed out of attempts to identify local leaders systematically, to characterize the structure of their interaction, and to understand the ways in which decisions affecting the locality are made, with or without their influence. While at times the field has been divided over the methodology to be used, recent research increasingly agrees that it is necessary to consider both reputational leaders and the actual participants in decisionmaking. The following discussion reflects this

171

trend, and attempts to provide operational criteria for
a more inclusive identification of the leaders and their
interaction in making certain decisions and avoiding
others.

The Site

These procedures have been brought to bear on the
process of economic development as it is being carried
out in the state of Jalisco, Mexico, particularly in the
area of Guadalajara, the state's capital. Guadalajara
was chosen as the site for this research because it
reflects both the progress and the persistent problems of
Mexico's development. It is Mexico's second largest
city, with a population nearing 1,300,000 in 1968. Yet
it is only recently that Guadalajara has begun to experience the rapid economic development characteristic of
Monterrey and the Federal District. In many respects
this growth has resulted from the same determined efforts
as those made by the federal government in collaboration
with local leaders in such cities as Puebla, Querétaro,
Salamanca and San Luis Potosi.

While any of these developing cities would have provided an instructive site, Guadalajara was selected
because its size and location, some 350 miles northwest
of Mexico City, provide an illustration of problems characteristic of the rest of the country. The economies of
the border towns are heavily influenced by tourist traffic; Monterrey and the Federal District have experienced
impressive industrial growth. But Guadalajara reflects
the problems and achievements of the country as a whole.
Some of the problems are: a structural dependence on
primary products; rapid urban migration with attendant
deficits in employment and urban services; unproductive
channeling of capital into property and rentals; centralization of financial and administrative power in the
Federal District; and a nascent industry struggling with
capital scarcities and an unfavorable balance of foreign
exchange.

Until the 1940's, Guadalajara was a commercial center and distribution point for the surrounding agricultural region. But since the second World War, the agri-
culturally based economy has begun to industrialize. The
annual growth rate of the industrial sector in recent
years has been 11.6 percent while the national average
was 7.8 percent. In 1967 the construction and transformation industries contributed 23 percent of the state's
gross product, a figure almost identical to that for
agricultural and livestock production. Commerce and services continue to dominate, contributing 45 percent of
the gross product. Industry is small and medium scale,
devoted principally to food products, textiles, shoes,
paper and chemicals. That is, it revolves around the
industrialization of agricultural products.

In 1967, 46 percent of the economically active population were occupied in primary activities; 24 percent in
industry; and 31 percent in commerce, services and transportation. Among Mexico's 29 states, two territories and
one federal district, Jalisco ranks in the middle third
in terms of aggregate value of industrial production per
capita. Population estimates for the state (in 1967)
were 3,300,072, with 2,195,661 urban and 1,104,411
rural.[1] The city of Guadalajara includes 1,263,269 persons, approximately double the number registered in 1957
and perhaps four times the population of 1945.

In other respects, Guadalajara is an important center of communication between the Federal District and the
entire northwest of the country. It boasts four universities and a generally higher level of education than
most Mexican cities. Like all of Mexico, Guadalajara is
staunchly Roman Catholic. Beyond that, it is reputed to
be a bastion of church conservatism in a nominally anti-
clerical country, and it includes the diocese of Mexico's
only cardinal. On a broader scale, it has a reputation
for being more "traditional" than most large Mexican
cities.

Finally, the city's temperate climate and pleasant surroundings have attracted a large North American community, and there are branch plants of such companies as Kodak, Phillip Morris, Burroughs, Union Carbide, Motorola and Corn Products. A number of absentee-owned firms from Monterrey and Mexico City are also represented.

Data Collection Methods

Our study employed several data gathering techniques: (1) interviews with persons occupying important positions in public and private organizations that dealt directly with questions of economic development; (2) interviews with persons whom the "positional" leaders most frequently nominated as influential in the economy; (3) case studies of decisionmaking and participation in five "activity areas." Here too, the activity areas were those the positional leaders thought most important to the development of the area. Interviewing remained the principal method in this phase, but was supplemented by observation of group activities and analysis of published material on the social, political and economic conditions of the area.

This three-stage procedure began with interviewing persons termed "subleaders," from those institutions, both public and private, concerned with economic development. The subleader sample included 65 people: 32 from the private sector, e.g., heads of organizations of industrialists, bankers, the Chamber of Commerce; and 33 from the public sector, e.g., heads of public agencies in charge of planning, credit, agriculture and urban services.[2]

The second series of interviews dealt with a group of persons we shall refer to as "influentials." They were selected on the basis of interview nominations by subleaders. When the first stage of interviewing was completed, all persons nominated as important in development activities were ranked by the number of nominations

received. A noticeable break appeared at the point of
five or more nominations. This was used as a cutoff
point.[3] The procedure yielded 19 influentials, of whom
15 were interviewed.

The third stage was analysis of the five most important examples of activity promoting local economic development. These areas, or events, were selected on the
basis of responses to the question, "What would you consider to be the most important projects or specific
activities related to the development of the area that
have been carried out in recent years or are actually
being carried out now?" Responses were coded in terms of
the general area of activity and specific projects within
the area. In the five most frequently mentioned areas,
specific activities were selected for study on the basis
of their representativeness, manageability and frequency
of mention.[4]

While both subleaders and influentials were given
the same structured interview, unstructured interviews
were administered to those identified as participants in
the five case studies. These interviewees, nominated by
the first two groups or by other activity participants,
were asked about the history of the project or activity,
important decisions and other actors. Twenty-five persons were interviewed at this stage, bringing the total
number of interviewees to 105.

THE STRUCTURE OF POWER: SUBLEADERS,
INFLUENTIALS AND GROUPS

As we attempt to discover the organization and constituency of Guadalajara's economic power structure, we
focus first on the people and groups regarded as influential. Because the subleaders are representative of the
economic community, it will be of interest to examine
this group and the way it compares with the influentials
in terms of reputation, background and attitudes.

TABLE I

INFLUENTIALS BY OCCUPATION AND NUMBER OF NOMINATIONS RECEIVED FROM PUBLIC AND PRIVATE SECTOR SUBLEADERS AND OTHER INFLUENTIALS

Occupation	Nominations received from			
	Private sector subleaders	Public sector subleaders	Other influentials	Totals
1. Governor of state	12	12	7	31
2. Industrialist--shoes	11	4	6	21
3. Banker	8	5	6	19
4. Industrialist--metals	10	1	7	18
5. Head of Dept. of Economy	7	7	3	17
6. Industrialist--foods	10	1	5	16
7. Industrialist--beverages	6	3	5	14
8. Treasurer of state	4	4	6	14
9. Industrialist--foods	5	2	6	13
10. Industrialist--textiles	3	1	4	8
11. Industrialist--construction	3	2	2	7
12. Industrialist--construction	3	1	3	7
13. Industrialist--metals	4	0	3	7
14. Industrialist--chemicals	3	1	3	7
15. Mayor of Guadalajara	3	2	1	6
16. Industrialist--foods	4	0	1	5
17. Industrialist--construction	3	1	1	5
18. Director--planning agency	1	3	1	5
19. Businessman--chain stores	2	2	1	5

Reputations for Leadership

Table I shows how subleaders and influentials perceive their own influence. The governor of the state is considered to be the most important participant in economic development. Additional nominees from the official sector include the head of the state department of economy, the state treasurer, the mayor of Guadalajara and the director of a regional development agency. Apart from these, the list is heavily weighted toward industrialists. The two remaining influentials are from banking and commerce. The occupational composition of the influentials is especially important when we remember that industry is neither the state's principal employer nor the principal contributor to the area's production. The data suggest that Guadalajara's power structure is a coalition of state officials and industrialists, with the larger share of power resting with the governor and his top lieutenants.

Table II indicates that organizations with reputations for influence in development work reflect the same institutional interests. Three of the top five are the Chamber of Commerce, the industrial chambers and the Bankers' Association. The Jalisco Institute for Promotion and Economic Studies and the Coordinating Junta of Private Initiative are outgrowths of the first three. Both were created to coordinate and more aggressively develop the region. The second six groups represent the official sector; unlike the ranking shown in Table I we do not find public sector representatives high on the list. This may not be inconsistent, for the interview asked for important "organizations," suggesting private groups rather than government agencies.

One important aspect of both tables is the relatively high agreement between subleaders and influentials. Although it is not apparent from the tables, the number of persons nominated by subleaders drops off rapidly after the cutoff. In only one case did influentials differ from subleaders with respect to whom they would include in their ranks. It is difficult to say

TABLE II

INFLUENTIAL ORGANIZATIONS BY NUMBER OF NOMINATIONS RECEIVED
FROM PUBLIC AND PRIVATE SECTOR SUBLEADERS AND INFLUENTIALS

| Name | Nominations received from | | | |
	Public sector subleaders	Private sector subleaders	Influentials	Totals
1. Chamber of Commerce	20	15	9	44
2. Industrial chambers	19	12	8	39
3. Jalisco Institute for Promotion and Economic Studies	16	4	3	23
4. Bankers' Association	4	10	3	17
5. Coordinating Junta of Private Initiative	8	4	5	17
6. Employers' Association	8	4	3	15
7. State Dept. of Economy	6	5	1	12
8. PRI (political party)	3	7	0	10
9. CROC (labor union)	2	8	0	10
10. CTM (labor union)	2	7	0	9
11. State government	3	2	0	5
12. Urbanization and Planning Dept. of state government	2	3	0	5

how many the influentials might have excluded for only
a small number made nominations. It was therefore difficult to set a cutoff. As Table I shows, five of the
influentials received only one vote from their fellows.
The maximum, however, is only seven (mean 3.6). A higher
nomination rate might have reduced the number of
"influentials' influentials," but it is unlikely that the
higher rate would have altered the constituency of that
smaller group. In the case of organizations, the same
situation obtains.

Tentatively, both tables suggest that the economic
power structure is directed by top political leaders
working in conjunction with prominent representatives of
the industrial, banking and commercial communities.

Social Background

Table III contrasts the socioeconomic level of
respondents with that of their fathers. It shows that
subleaders are primarily from middle socioeconomic
stratum. The influentials, on the other hand, are
almost exclusively from the upper group. Because these
differences are partly a consequence of the sampling procedure, the question of mobility arouses greater interest. Among the subleaders, fathers were predominantly
from the lower stratum, especially in the case of public
sector subleaders. In contrast, the fathers of influentials were more often from the middle and upper strata.

Table IV indicates that upward mobility is the rule
for public sector subleaders and influentials. Private
sector subleaders are evenly divided between the upwardly
mobile and stable categories. Downward mobility is
extremely rare, and many of the people in the stable
category have been vertically mobile.

Ideological Attitudes

A number of interview questions sought to elicit
ideological attitudes. Although Mexico has four legally

TABLE III

Public and Private Sector Subleaders and Influentials
By Socioeconomic Strata and Socioeconomic
Strata of Fathers

	Socioeconomic strata			
	Upper	Middle	Lower	Totals
Private sector				
subleaders	9	23	1	33
fathers	7	10	15	32
Public sector				
subleaders	3	28	0	31
fathers	1	14	16	31
Influentials	14	1	0	15
Fathers	5	7	3	15

TABLE IV

Social Mobility of Public and Private Sector
Subleaders and Influentials

	Mobility			
	Upward	Stationary	Downward	Totals
Private sector				
subleaders	16	16	1	33
Public sector				
subleaders	18	12	1	31
Influentials	9	6	0	15

recognized political parties, it is essentially a one-
party state: the PRI (*Partido Revolucionario Institu-
cional*) enjoys the vast preponderance of public support.
For this reason, we did not rely on party identification,
but sought a wider variety of responses by asking the
person to describe himself in terms of his political

attitudes and principles. The results, which appear in
Table V, demonstrate that leaders are either supporters
of the system or consider themselves apolitical.

TABLE V

Political Identification of Public and Private
Sector Subleaders and Influentials

	PRI and the Mexican System	Apolitical	Opposition Party	Totals
Private sector subleaders	11	9	1	21
Public sector subleaders	13	6	1	20
Influentials	9	6	0	15

The latter category is especially interesting. We
found that a frequent response was "I am not a *politico*,
I am a *technico*." To be "political" carries the connota-
tion of having political ambitions within the PRI system;
conversely, to be apolitical implies other career ambitions. The system itself is not a debatable matter:
many respondents observed that the government and PRI
were doing a good job running the country, which is,
after all, their business. In short, the existing system
has basic acceptance and support, ranging from passive
approval to active enthusiasm, largely on the part of
officials whose careers depend upon their standing in the
party.[6]

Other studies have revealed ideological attitudes
through questions about the appropriate scope and limits
of governmental activity.[7] Following this approach,
leaders were asked if they thought Mexico's economic
development would proceed better under free enterprise or
under a system of governmental control of the means of
production. Table VI shows that while little opposition

TABLE VI

Attitudes of Public and Private Sector Subleaders
and Influentials Toward Free Enterprise v.
Government Control of the Economy

	Unqualified support of free enterprise	Government intervention necessary	Totals
Private sector subleaders	11	20	31
Public sector subleaders	2	22	24
Influentials	1	6	7

to free enterprise was expressed, most respondents felt
that governmental intervention in the economy was necessary and beneficial. The only departure from this attitude came from that third of the private sector subleaders-
ers who endorsed free enterprise without qualification.
This is another indication of the ideological unanimity
that characterizes Guadalajara leaders.

THE PROCESS OF DEVELOPMENT DECISIONMAKING

Summary of Case Studies

Using the procedure outlined earlier, the five
activity or decision areas identified as most important
for the recent development of the area were: (1) infrastructure works, e.g., highways, electrification, natural
gas, airports; (2) economic planning; (3) urbanization,
i.e., growth in urban services; (4) industrial promotion;
and (5) agricultural development. Because space does not
allow detailed treatment of each of these areas, some
general observations will suffice.

Mexico's financial and administrative organization
is highly centralized: effective local action demands
that local leaders be able to command the attention of
high federal officials. One of the most effective ways

to accomplish this is to communicate a spirit of united
dedication to local development upwards to the federal
level. Such a spirit exists in Guadalajara. In the
areas of infrastructure and industrial promotion, state
and local agencies often work with the private sector
through industrial and commercial chambers. A new air-
port and natural gas viaduct are cases in point, where
unified local initiative won federal financial backing
for these projects. In these and other cases, the state
government usually occupies the principal leadership
role. There are also cases in which the private sector
initiates projects, but these too require official backing for success. A major dimension of the structure of
power, then, is the active collaboration of public and
private agencies in development projects.

Two additional characteristics are apparent as we
look at the organization of the public and private sectors separately. The Mexican public sector, particularly
at the policy-making level, consists largely of professional politicians working their way up in the party.
Their careers depend to a great extent on their reputations as promoters of progressive change. This, in turn,
depends on their ability to satisfy a broad constituency
of students, farmers, labor and businessmen, simultaneously while maintaining political peace. The latter
task, significant in itself, may hinder economic development. In an area without major electoral competition,
public upheaval, including the dissatisfaction of
influential segments, is the principal method of replac-
ing a public official. Thus incumbents seek to avoid
dissatisfaction, frequently at the cost of development
programs. The case studies indicated several areas in
which state support of development projects was constrained by the need to maintain peace: low income public housing is lagging, due to the opposition of a strong
construction industry; only limited resources are being
channeled into agricultural development because of the
disproportionate influence of the industrial and commercial sectors.

Private development projects are similarly constrained by the organization of power. Interviewees frequently commented that egoism and traditionalism hindered
development efforts that required mutual confidence and
large-scale cooperation. Our case studies support this
observation. We found that most of Guadalajara's enter-
prises are not public corporations, but are family owned
and operated; investment in joint capital ventures is
limited relative to the size of savings accounts; appeals
by public officials for increased investment are generally unsuccessful; and those who do invest prefer the
security of private real estate holdings to the risks of
industrial ventures.

These characteristics have important consequences
for political power. Splits are increasing within the
private sector; the alliance between the chambers themselves is uneasy. The Chamber of Commerce, parent of
all the others, has lost much of the power it once held
as sole representative of the private sector. The industrial chambers have become independent. To avoid further
deterioration of its position, the Chamber of Commerce
has opposed plans of the Coordinating Junta, and the
question of leadership has split the industrial chambers
themselves into two factions. These conflicts have
reduced the effectiveness of private sector planning
efforts.

In summary, the case studies suggest three generalizations concerning the organization of power: (1) public-
private cooperation is relatively extensive; (2) organizational fission is occurring in the private sector; and
(3) the power of the public sector is constrained by the
need to maintain political peace. These characteristics
help account for the scope and effectiveness of develop-
mental decisions.

Leaders

Because many people participated in each of the
decision areas, some method for designating the principal

actors had to be established. The problem is a complex
one, with no entirely satisfactory solution. Our criterion defined an important actor in any single area as
an individual who was so identified by the known participants whom we had interviewed.[8]

In this way, we determined the principal participants in each area covered by a case study. The pool of
names was then compared with Table I in order to determine the congruence of the two methods. We then introduced a final term, "leaders," to refer to those people
who qualified as important on the basis of a composite
criterion. Specifically, a "leader" was an individual:
(1) nominated as an influential and active in at least
one decision area; or (2) active in two or more decision
areas.

Table VII identifies these leaders and the scope of
their influence. Six persons active in two or more decision areas are thus added to our first approximation,
while two inactive influentials are dropped. These 23
leaders are a reasonably complete and representative
sample of the individuals most active in Guadalajara's
development. We do not claim that the list is exhaus-
tive; other equally important individuals were probably
not identified because their activities were less well
known.[9] Our group, however, includes all of the key
leaders.

Further, this group is representative of the structural characteristics and the location of power in Guadalajara. Nearly all of the leaders are affiliated with
organizations listed as important in Table II. This
point should be emphasized. Power structures are too
often conceived in terms of autonomous actors, wielding
personal power and whose associations are based on real-
izing personal goals. Our results suggest a more sociological interpretation in which power resides in a social
structure constituted by the interrelations of institutions and the men who represent them. In more substantive terms, power in Guadalajara resides in a coalition
of interests headed by the state governor, the chief link

TABLE VII

GUADALAJARA LEADERS AND AREAS OF PARTICIPATION

Position	Areas of participation[a]
1. Governor of state	1, 2, 3, 4, 5
2. Industrialist--shoes	1, 4
3. Banker	1, 4
4. Industrialist--metals	1, 4
5. Head of Dept. of Economy	1, 2, 4
6. Industrialist--foods	4
7. Industrialist--beverages	1, 4
8. Treasurer of state	1, 2, 3, 4
9. Industrialist--foods	4
10. Industrialist--construction	3, 4
11. Industrialist--construction	1, 3, 4
12. Industrialist--metals	4
13. Industrialist--chemicals	4
14. Industrialist--construction	1, 3
15. Director--planning agency	2, 5
16. Businessman--chain stores	4
17. Mayor of Guadalajara	3
18. Director--private planning institute	1, 2, 4
19. Ex-Governor and Federal Minister	1, 3, 5
20. Businessman--restaurants	2, 4
21. Businessman--automobiles	1, 3
22. Industrialist--foods	1, 3
23. Public relations and governor aid	1, 4

[a]
1. Infrastructure	4. Industrial promotion
2. Economic planning	5. Agricultural development
3. Urbanization	

to the all-important federal government. Within this coalition, the state government actively collaborates with the industrial, banking and commercial communities. The leaders are persons who represent these institutions and work actively for the realization of their interests.

SOCIAL ORGANIZATION AND ECONOMIC DEVELOPMENT: SOME CONCLUSIONS

Our study indicates several ways in which the social organization of Guadalajara's economic power structure affects the state's capacity to promote economic development.

1. In institutional terms, the organization of power is close-knit: a relatively small number of collaborating organizations, and their representatives, are regarded as influential. These organizations actually do work together in a regularized fashion on projects of mutual interest.

2. Simultaneously, a separatist tendency is evident in the private sector, particularly among those further from the centers of decisionmaking. This tendency seems to be rooted in the self-sufficient tradition of an agrarian, property-based economy.

3. In the public sector, similar deterrents to cooperation arise from the need to preserve harmony at the expense of development programs. This is, of course, true of all political systems. But Mexico's ruling party, in order to preserve its popular base, seems to engage in rather elaborate concessionary practices.

4. Leaders and subleaders in Guadalajara's economic community are an ideologically cohesive group.

5. If the organization of power is a coalition of government, industrial, banking and commercial interests, it is also one in which the public sector is clearly the most decisive component. It is a publicly directed coalition.

6. The power structure consists of an open, mobile elite. It is an elite, in that joint actions are undertaken by a small and privileged group of persons who are personally and institutionally interconnected. The elite is open: no special economic or social barriers are raised against potential entrants. Most members have, in fact, been socially mobile.

7. The administratively centralized, single party regional structure reflects the organization of power at the federal level. The federal system demands parallel organization on the regional level, for local activities must be closely articulated with the federal system.

8. Political and administrative centralism also affects the form in which power is exercised locally: public and private organizations collaborate to attract a larger share of federal funds.

REFLECTIONS

Finally, let us consider how this exploratory research can help reformulate the orientation presented in the foregoing paper. These reflections have two purposes; first to assess the strengths and weaknesses of the theoretical scheme; second to indicate some of the difficulties that may arise in organizing the theoretical structure for power research.

As the first three of the preceding observations indicate, the integration of power is a more complex concept than we had anticipated. Our case studies suggest at least two types of integration. One has to do with "levels"--the size of the units integrated. Thus we found that institutional integration may coexist with group and individual separatism. But the extent of separatism limits the range of institutional collaboration. Next is the question of "distance" from the center of decision-making activities, i.e., integration, may be extensive or intensive. These two types may have different consequences on the integrated unit's capacity for action.

With respect to point four above, although ideological diversity is often said to aid the decision-making process, our case studies suggest that unanimity was important in promoting joint projects between public and private institutions. Unfortunately, our cases do not allow much speculation on the consequences of diversity.

Our fifth observation tends to support the hypothesis of the inequality of power. The public sector's unequivocal leadership minimizes veto power and necessitates a particular style of reaching and executing decisions. On the other hand, the numerous factions in influential circles, as well as the openness and mobility of the elite (noted in point six), reflect a relatively broad distribution of power. Most of the private sector is represented; the public sector, due to its political dependence, represents a broad constituency. No single clique dominates, but the state government is both arbiter and executive. The fact that this arrangement coopts many segments into support for development programs verifies our earlier speculation on the consequences of the distribution of power.

The last two summary statements point to a deficiency in our theoretical orientation. Clearly, we must devote a great deal more attention to the relations between levels of social organization (local-national or national-international). In the present case, the local power arrangement gained efficiency as a result of its structural and ideological similarity to the national structure.

All these observations help point the way toward a reformulation of the original approach. In the case of Guadalajara's economic development, the factor most responsible for directed change was the capacity for collaborative action in decisionmaking. In short, the exploratory study has helped to concretize a key process or "intervening variable." Similarly, it has suggested a number of circumstances promoting this capacity for collaborative action: (1) power inequality, and a necessity for collaboration; (2) legitimacy of leading

institutions; (3) a broad distribution of power, combined
with opportunities to enter positions of decision-making
responsibility; (4) extensive ideological support; and
(5) close articulation with superordinate systems.

NOTES

[1] The Mexican census follows the North American convention of designating as "urban" any locality with over 2,500 inhabitants.

[2] This group of 65 exhausts nearly all positions in development-related institutions, although it was reduced by a 10 to 15 percent refusal rate. Further, several members of the first sample later proved to be influentials and were counted in that group.

[3] In contrast to U.S. studies, this cutoff point is quite low, but was judged necessary due to a marked reluctance to "name names." This is undoubtedly a cultural factor with a variety of explanations, all of which create difficulties for power structure research in Mexico.

[4] In order to systematically establish a focus for the study of participation and overt exercise of influence, the responses of interviewees concerning important development activities were first tabulated. A wide variety of "events" were recorded, ranging from very specific projects to general changes (probes used in the interviews to elicit specific responses were not always successful). Next, these responses were grouped into decision areas that would reflect both the most important activities and a broad spectrum of decisionmaking. Accordingly, while infrastructure works were the most frequently mentioned projects, it was decided not to study highways and electrification separately. Early indications were that such a procedure would have resulted in examination of a series of activities realized in roughly the same manner. Rather, infrastructure was designated as one of five areas selected to obtain a broader and more representative picture of the entire decision-making process.

[5] The categories employed here included the following
occupations: upper--owners and top executives of large
corporations, top governmental posts (governor, mayor,
cabinet jobs), medical doctors; middle--lawyers, directors
of public and private agencies, party functionaries,
medium and small business owners, bankers, public employees, large-scale farmers; lower--small and tenant
farmers, shopkeepers, tradesmen. Useful sources on
social class in Latin America have been collected in
Joseph A. Kahl, ed., *La Industialización en América
Latina* (Mexico: Fondo de Cultura Económica, 1965).

[6] As the table indicates, uncodable responses presented
a problem. The procedure was not entirely successful,
though it led to some interesting results, such as this
one.

[7] Robert E. Agger et al., *The Rulers and the Ruled:
Political Power and Impotence in American Communties* (New
York: John Wiley and Sons, 1964).

[8] This problem has not been adequately treated in the
literature on the decision-making method of identifying
leaders. While actual participation is stressed as the
best indicator of who really has power, an operational
definition of what constitutes "significant participation" is seldom found. I see no easy solution to the
problem other than trying to get as complete a history of
the activity as possible and then taking a consensus of
views. Thus, at some point we must accept "reputational"
evidence with this method.

[9] On an impressionistic basis these would include: an
attorney active in commerce, an architect influential in
public works, another ex-governor in the Federal Cabinet,
the present governor's first secretary, a realtor and
large property holder, and three other industrialists.

Discussion: Session I
Dallas, Texas

chaired by FREDERICK M. WIRT

EDITOR'S NOTE

The Dallas symposium was followed by a brief discussion period. As the following pages indicate, the participants, even though limited by time, raised some interesting questions about the methodology needed to implement comparative studies.

On April 15, 1968, the discussion continued in Austin, giving both speakers and members of the audience an opportunity to pursue these questions further. An especially useful feature of the Austin session was Terry N. Clark's introduction, summarizing the earlier proceedings for the benefit of a partially new audience. Clark's comments have been reproduced as a separate essay, between the two discussion transcripts.

THE DALLAS DISCUSSION

Comment from audience: One thing that struck me was that the U.S. Census Bureau could start gathering data along the lines needed in our research.

Scoble: Yes, I would like to second that. I learned just before I came here that four of the *County and City Data Books* are now on magnetic tape. I think these are 1952, 1957, 1962 and 1967. If we can get some decent political variables along with the economic and demographic variables, comparative analysis would be speeded up tremendously.

Wirt: This would be most helpful in following up Amos Hawley's article on urban renewal policy and power distributions.

Scoble: Before he left NORC, Peter Rossi did create a panel. His idea was to have a panel of the 200 largest cities in the United States, with a resident social scientist in each. He would pick up precisely the total vote cast for the winning party in the presidential election in that city. Then we would have more explicitly political variables, ones we don't now find in either the *County and City Data Book* or the *Municipal Year Book*. [Ed. note: For a fuller description of this project, see Rossi and Robert Crain, "The NORC Permanent Community Sample," *Public Opinion Quarterly*, 32(2): 261-272 (1968).]

Bonjean: Let me add that we have recently conducted a study in Austin for which we took most of the data from the *County and City Data Book*. We supplemented it with data from [Scammon's] *America Votes* and ran it all through a factor analysis. It's starting at the opposite end from where some of us started today. The political variables weren't too closely associated with any of the economic and demographic variables. I'd be glad to send a copy to any of you who are interested in what we found.

Comment from audience: This is directed toward Professor Adrian. What is your definition of "power" and "power structure?"

Adrian: I said I didn't think that I knew. My point was that we still do not have agreement on the meaning of either "power" or "structure" as they are used in that sense. I think that is clear from the difference between the way Dr. Hunter refers to "power" and the way I refer to it. That is, he says that power is a process. I can't conceive of it as a process. To me decisionmaking is the process that we are concerned with, and power is an agglomeration of resources that may or may not be used in making particular decisions. We don't all have to use the same definitions, but I think we often ignore the definitions. Frequently we leave them implicit. Then when we criticize one another's work, we are confronted with the old apples and oranges problem.

Comment from audience: I think some recent problems with urban renewal and the poverty program in Fort Worth show that the power structure within the Chamber of Commerce is not the real power structure. In many political and social areas I don't think we pick up all the leaders unless we go beyond financial leaders. That has certainly shown up in our community: the Chamber of Commerce members may be the financial leaders, but they cannot be the total political leaders.

Wirt: There is a more general question here: the total impact on power structures of massive federal funding. One hundred million dollars per year comes into Oakland for neighborhood poverty programs. What does this do to existing structures?

Adrian: This is one way to look at the total picture. In Oakland it isn't as interesting to investigate who wants another Bay Bridge as it is to study who is trying to prevent the Black nationalists from burning the place to the ground next summer--and if not next summer then the summer after that. Many questions of social policy are extremely diffuse and long range. Yet they are so central to national and local public policy that we cannot say they are outside the scope of critical decisionmaking in the community. In fact, they are the *essence* of it. It is legitimate to say that one cannot or does not wish to study such an issue. But it is not legitimate to conclude that the issue is therefore irrelevant.

Scoble: I believe it's wrong to totally exclude the possibility of economic determinism. One of the things political scientists do constantly is to deny the relevance of social class to power. But we should take into our accounting of schemes of community power structure studies the possibility that there are some cities where economic and traditional commercial-financial interests do call the shots. This may be true of Atlanta, which is a growth center for a five-state region. But there may be others with a long-standing two-party system, where the independent political leader has considerably more power. Maybe Dahl's New Haven is prototypical here--old New England where the ethnic minorities have been absorbed fairly well. But I don't think we ought to throw out the first possibility at all.

Clark: As Harry Scoble pointed out, Peter Rossi and Bob Crain were instrumental in involving the National Opinion Research Center in the large-scale study of community decisionmaking. (I came to the University of Chicago the same year that Peter Rossi left.) The project was continued as a joint undertaking of the International Studies of Values in Politics and the NORC Permanent Community Sample. In January 1967, we collected data on community decisionmaking in a national sample of 51 communities. We are presently analyzing these materials in conjunction with data from the *County and City Data Book*, *The Municipal Year Book*, and similar sources. [Ed. note: The study is discussed on pp. 49ff.] We have been trying to isolate the economic, political, demographic and cultural determinants of centralized or pluralistic decision-making patterns. We have also tried to relate decision-making patterns to policy outputs, a question that was under discussion today. Thus I would like to ask Harry Scoble and anyone else who would like to comment: How can we examine--more systematically than has been done thus far in most of the literature--the relationships between decision-making patterns and policy outputs? How can we first measure and then explain the degree to which various actors involved in the process of decisionmaking are advantaged or disadvantaged by various decisions?

Scoble: I think this is almost impossible without independent social accounting agencies. Alford and I analyzed four Wisconsin cities that had a fairly good municipal tradition, clean cities, clean in their political organizations. We tried to collect output data for these four cities and found that the existing data were totally inadequate. Even the *Municipal Year Book* is no good. I think you have to define a series of questions, such as per capita input for child education and the median starting salary for new school teachers. Then data must be collected independently; reliable data do not come from city hall.

Reflections on the Symposium

by TERRY N. CLARK

and

Discussion: Session II
Austin, Texas

Anyone who reviews a session such as the one that took place in Dallas inevitably forms his own *gestalt*. My interpretation may well differ from that of others. But although each of us might present a somewhat different picture of the conference, I doubt that there would be as many presentations as there were participants. Let me review a few of the themes that struck me as particularly important.

Perhaps my most significant impression of the Dallas meetings is one of consensus. Not a consensus in the sense of unanimity, for such consensus seldom emerges in rapidly changing intellectual disciplines. If one did, it would probably be more stultifying than productive. Nevertheless, there was an underlying agreement on several issues that would not have been present five or 10 years ago in such a meeting. There were important similarities in the definition of basic problems and in the directions in which solutions are being sought. In this respect, the conference paralleled recent developments in the literature on community decisionmaking.

But what can we say more specifically about this emerging consensus? One important aspect was the virtual absence of the old debate over whether American communities are fundamentally monolithic or pluralistic. Nor did the question of whether a "power structure" exists warrant spending much time on it. There was little ad hoc generalization from single community research. And the need for a more systematic and coherent theory of community decisionmaking was recognized.

Finally, the speakers stressed the need for large-scale empirical research on numerous communities. Such comparative research helps destroy the ethnocentrisms that arise from the study of a single community, or, in the case of cross-national research, from national stereotypes. Floyd Hunter discussed the ease of analyzing

large quantities of data with modern computers. John
Walton has been working in Mexico and is going to Colombia; Delbert Miller has been working in Argentina; I have
been collaborating with researchers in Yugoslavia and
France. Several other cross-national comparative studies
are also in progress. In addition, there is a continuing
effort to integrate the discrete findings that emerge
from individual community studies and to formulate a
slightly more general--if you will, middle level or
upper middle range--theory. Adrian and Walton both
emphasized this tendency.

We can also go beyond this sort of general statement
and suggest the kinds of variables we want in such a middle level theory, as well as the general framework we
need to work with. We can summarize this in a diagram
like Figure I. First, there is an important emphasis on
"community structural characteristics." These can be
broken down into demographic, economic, legal-political
and cultural, all of which are specific to the local community. Because no community is completely isolated,
perhaps we should include a factor we might call "inputs
to the community." These would be closely related to the
characteristics of the state, region and national society.
All these are basically independent variables. We can
then examine their impact on two variables that have been
the focus of a good deal of discussion and debate: (1)
the decision-making structure of the community, monolithic or pluralistic, centralized or decentralized; and
(2) the type of leadership. The latter is distinct from
the structure of leadership, which includes the values of
the leaders, their attitudes and beliefs, and their
social background. All these variables largely determine
the "outputs" that emerge from community decisions. We
can formalize the relationships among the variables by
connecting them with a series of arrows. Much of the
emerging theory can, in fact, be considered as attempts
to specify whether there should be plus or minus signs on
the different arrows. We should eventually be able to
subsume the specific arrows and plus or minus signs

FIGURE I

BASIC VARIABLES IN COMMUNITY DECISIONMAKING

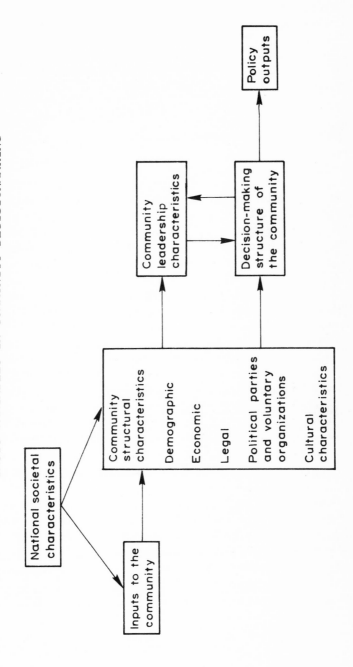

connecting distinct variables under a few general propositions.[1]

One of the problems in carrying out such a program is the difficulty of measuring the centralization of decisionmaking. This is a problem familiar to all of us. Leaving specific solutions aside for the moment, I think it is fair to say that many persons in the field agree that methods must be comparable from one community and one study to the next. This is particularly important as increasingly larger and more expensive studies are undertaken.

In the study of 51 American communities presently underway at the University of Chicago, we tried to adapt some of the best research methods from earlier studies in the field.[2] These same basic methods have been adapted for use in Yugoslavia and France.

Let me now move to the leadership box. Harry Scoble has emphasized the social mobility of leaders, as well as the effects of upward or downward mobility on leaders' value orientations. That is, whether the reference group of leaders is their membership group or their group of origin, is important in determining how they will act in community decisions. Charles Bonjean stressed the importance of leaders' values and told of the attitude scales he has been administering to leaders in Texas communities. This is an important step, but I wonder to what degree these methods enable the civic culture of a community to be portrayed, as it was in Adrian and Williams' *Four Cities*, and in Agger, Goldrich and Swanson's volume.[3]

[1] See Terry N. Clark, ed., *Community Structure and Decision-Making: Comparative Analyses* (San Francisco: Chandler, 1968).

[2] The methods in the 51-city study are discussed on pp. 49ff.

[3] Robert E. Agger, Daniel Goldrich and Bert E. Swanson, *The Rulers and the Ruled* (New York: John Wiley and Sons, 1964).

In our 51-community study we tried to reveal the
civic culture by asking our informants to what degree the
community was oriented toward goals such as Adrian and
Williams outlined. But although our informants were the
best we could find in a cross-section of American
communities--mayor, newspaper editor, bar association
president, leading banker, and the like--their responses
were generally worthless. The agreement among respondents within a single community was too low for us to
construct a meaningful measure for the community as a
whole. Perhaps we should wait a few more years; when all
community influentials have read *Four Cities*, they can
simply tell us which type their community actually is.
But for the present, and for those leaders in backwater
towns who may never see the book, it would be useful if
we could find some alternative. Although I hesitate to
suggest such stringent measures it may even be necessary
to formulate other types of civic culture. I would be
interested in suggestions from Charles Adrian or anyone
else on this problem.

On a more general conceptual level, I was interested
in Adrian's remarks on power as a consumption item which
is difficult to replenish. I have not seen his actual
paper, but it seemed close enough to some other efforts
in this area to constitute what Robert Merton has called
a multiple discovery.[4]

While I could comment on other themes that were
raised in Dallas, my present task is to open the discussion, not to close it. For this reason, I will conclude
with a series of questions that seem central to present
and future research on community power and decisionmaking. Perhaps some of the panel members will have
thoughts on how to answer these and other questions.

One perennial problem is the construction of a more
accurate measure of centralization of decisionmaking. I
think that our "issue specific reputational" and "ersatz

---

[4]Clark, note 1 above, Chapter 3.

decisional" methods are fundamentally sound, but they can
be developed. For example, issues differ in importance.
Questions about urban renewal or mayoral election can be
asked in two different communities, but the "importance"
of the issues may not be equal. How is one to rank
importance? By the resources expended in the issue area?
By the resources redistributed--if a method of measurement can be found? Or by the importance that community
informants assign to issue areas?

A second general question deals with the dimensions
of leadership. What are the theoretically most significant dimensions we can use to analyze the complex series
of phenomena called "leadership"? The importance of any
particular dimension is measured ideally in terms of a
theoretical framework, such as I presented above. What
we ask, are the dimension's consequences for the empirical referents of other variables specified in the model?
Charles Bonjean touched on five important dimensions, but
are there others that we should include or elaborate further?

Let me also ask again: how are we to better conceptualize and measure community civic cultures? And how
can we better measure the benefits that accrue to various
individuals and subsectors of a community through particular decisions? How are direct and indirect benefits to
be distinguished? And short-term from long-term benefits?

But let me now pass the discussion to the panelists.

Adrian: You asked why efforts to measure images of
the community haven't worked out. I think the answer
comes from the guru of the current "in-group" in political science, David Easton, who says:

> Research clearly demonstrates the
> intrinsic difficulties in construct-
> ing the conceptual and technical
> tools for laying bare the roots of
> power. It is feasible and useful
> to talk of the politically relevant

members, even though they may be
presently indeterminate, as long as we
believe that in principle they are
empirically discoverable groups.

So long as we believe in scientific method, there is
always the chance that it will work. It seems to me that
if we look at where political science has been going in
this area since Dahl, we see that political science will
probably continue to be a holding company, rather than a
discipline. It is a holding company within which we look
at many things from many perspectives.

If there is any single focus emerging, it is political science as a study of strategies for using power.
We're increasingly interested in looking at how decision-
making coalitions are built at the local level. We have
to look at this because the power structure, which at one
time may have been essentially monolithic in many communities (and we have no reason to believe that it wasn't
or that in many communities it still isn't), seems to be
increasingly competitive today. This means, first, that
we must look at some of the developments in coalition
theory that have been building out of game theory, which
came to political science from economics. Second, it
raises some central questions about willingness to use
power, as opposed to the simple existence of power.

Perhaps we can use economics in some of our future
studies of community power; we can try to apply demand
theory to the decision process and to the use of power in
the community. I don't have time to go into this, but
one reason why we find so many nondecisions in the local
community has been that quite frequently the demand, say,
for adequate low-income housing has been high, but the
community power structure's willingness to expend
resources has been low, so low that there is no meeting
of the demand and supply curves. The result is a "nonde-
cision" in the community. In addition to this, we need
to know: Where do you arrive at potential decisions?
Where can you build a coalition that will make a decision? And what is the nature of the elasticity of demand

and supply for any service or commodity? Again this is a concept from economics and I'm not going to take the time to develop it, especially since many of you have had elementary economic theory.

This gets back to my earlier question about the measurement of behavior in various issue areas. Obviously, if we use the supply and demand approach, we do have to specify issue areas. In economics, you cannot look at a general demand curve; a demand curve must explain the demand for Studebakers or Fords or some other specific product. By borrowing this analogy from economics, we see once again the need to move in the direction of greater specificity of issue areas.

If we could measure the elasticity and extent of demand and supply, we would have better ideas about the willingness to expend resources in various issue areas. Perhaps we can tie this in with the need to find better ways of measuring the value of constructs in the community, or, as political scientists might be more inclined to say, the ideologies prevalent in the community. As I suggested in Dallas, the community can be viewed not as simply an ecology of games, as Norton Long has suggested, but also as an ecology of ideologies.

Finally, I would suggest that many past studies have assumed the relevance of community power, rather than demonstrating it. Of course, we have to assume that we are looking at something important, but I asked in the Dallas session whether the community power we can measure is relevant to the major political issues of the day. Of course it has some importance, but I suggest that we must increasingly look at power as a pattern of simultaneous interaction at three or more levels of government. Very often we have to understand the negative use of power-- power as a means of blocking groups and blocking action, through vetoes, delaying tactics, and the like. This is a very common thing in the pattern of cooperative federalism, which is often, of course, noncooperative federalism.

The important questions, then, are: First, who decides what is relevant? Second, on what issues is community political power a useful concept in explaining political behavior today? I suspect that if taken alone, it really measures a good deal less of the total political cal system than we once thought it would.

Clark: What you suggest is supported by our finding that decentralization of decisionmaking is not at all the strongest predictor of policy outputs. Decentralization leads to slightly higher general budget and urban renewal expenditures, but it is less important than certain community structural characteristics--such as form of government, economic diversification, the education and income of the population, and, to a striking degree, the percent of the population that is Catholic. Communities with large numbers of residents who are Catholics spend a good deal more on all forms of governmental activity.

Scoble: Let me butt in for just a minute on this. It seems to me there is another aspect of this that political scientists have been terribly simple-minded about, one that can be found in Presthus' *Men At the Top*. That is the assumption that by measuring the percentage overlap from one decisional area or issue area to another, some measure of pluralism is found. Let me give an example. If community A has a 20 percent overlap while 80 percent are single issue actors, and community B has a 40 percent overlap and 60 percent single issue actors, then we would assert that there is an important difference between city A and city B, that city B is more pluralistic than city A. But we have no test for this. We haven't even articulated the assumptions.

Clark: Does anyone else want to speak to this question? I recall it was mentioned by more than one person in Dallas.

Hunter: There is a very real question here in terms of studying one city after another, comparing their structures, and coming up with a picture of what makes

America tick. I am not against comparative studies. I
think they're doing some very interesting things, getting
at interesting variables, tying down some of the variables that may exist from one city to another. But
within the total structure of policymaking in our lives
today, we live in national systems of power. And the
national power structure, or power structures, in the
United States don't operate on the basis of the statistical variables that operate city to city. In essence, the
national system seems to operate on the basis of a kind
of coalition of the federal establishment with the sleazy
combination of political conservatives of the South and
the industrial anarchists and feudalists of the North.
You have to take that into account. And you have to know
that there are major corporations: *Fortune* magazine pub-
licizes some 500 of them every August or September. But
now those 500 are rapidly becoming 250.

And you have to think of communities as anchor
points of power. We live in an urban system in this
world, and the urban communities are anchor points of
power. There are people in New York who know people in
San Francisco, and there are people in San Francisco who
know people in Dallas. They know each other on a first-
name basis and according to a division of functions--
goods and services--between them, and they move goods and
services in definable ways. What I think I'm saying here
is that, along with a comparative analysis, we need to
elevate these community studies into the study of a
larger system of power.

I want to give a list now, since I have the floor,
of some of the questions I think are pertinent in terms
of this kind of study. How do we get peace, domestic and
foreign, in this national system of ours? Who is moving
in relation to this and how are they moving? How do we
rebuild the cities of America, and the slums and the
rural slums of America, rebuild them socially, politically and economically? How do we divide the booty more
equitably among the underlying populations, and finally
how do we divide the work load more equitably?

Walton: One of the most interesting things to come out of these meetings is that people are beginning to talk about the question of "Who benefits?" whether they call it "dividing up the booty" or "precipitation of benefits." And I think that this isn't a difficult problem in terms of technique.

In Mexico, after we used our methods and sampling and self-generating samples of leaders, we finally went to the Governor, who we knew all along was the one who pulled the strings in the area. We asked him where the money was being spent in the state, and he replied that it was going for electric and industrial gas projects. When I asked him what data he took into consideration in making this decision, he said, "I'm glad you asked me that because we have a whole room full of data here." We went into the room, and there were tallied the gross product of the state, the number of people employed, the median income level. The Governor explained that in view of all these advantages in the state, it could support industrial gas. "So we bring it in, and the one who benefits is the large scale industrialist. The guy who is making windows and lamps can't afford to pay for industrial gas. He buys crude oil and heats up his torch with that." So here is your system of allocating funds in the state, and here are the people who benefit from them, and this seems more or less straightforward. So I'd suggest that we introduce this type of consideration into our research and, ultimately, into our theorizing. It doesn't pose problems of technique.

Scoble: I'd like to jump in with a favorite plea. Bob Agger once wrote an article, "Political Research As/Is Political Action." The question of "Who benefits?" is not an easy question, for there is a difference between immediate and long-term beneficiaries. The poverty program, I would argue, is in the long-term interest of the economic and political elite of this society, even though the immediate benefits seem to go to poor people. But

this is an ideological question. You can't get away from
ideology in trying to reach conclusions about who benefits. I think this is the problem on which we're stuck.

Walton: It is "ideological" in the sense of understanding the problem on the part of those who are making
decisions. I think that dictates the type of solutions
they develop and their allocation of resources.

Scoble: What I am saying to political scientists is
that there cannot be a value-free political science. You
must face the ideological issues.

Stephens: I liked the term that was used earlier:
ecology of values. I think we have to recognize this
whenever we talk in terms of various levels of issues,
even within a metropolitan area. I also liked the point
that issues are more open now than ever before. At least
more people have access to various kinds of mechanisms
for putting things on the agenda. It is important to
know what things go on the agenda and which are relegated
to bureaucratic routine. When we talk about values and
benefits, we do have problems in measuring what they are,
whether they are short-term or long-term. I think one of
our problems is learning to analyze which issues or
values are important in a given community or in part of
a given community.

Clark: I know from what you have told us that you
moved in this direction in some of your own work, in
which you try to explain certain community outputs. Maybe this cannot tell us "Who benefits?" as directly as we
would like, but could you perhaps summarize a few of your
findings in terms of the impact of particular community
characteristics on policy outputs?

Stephens: I'm not sure I could. My own research
attempts to set up a typology of suburban communities,
then analyze the impact of such decisions as increases

or decreases in state aid on these communities' decisions. We find that some political folklore appears
erroneous. For instance, many dormitory suburbs tend to
benefit more than any other communities from such proposals as increasing state aid. The concept that better
metropolitan integration would be achieved if state aid
were abolished simply does not hold up. I'm not sure
that my findings are in any way definitive, but they do
indicate that some of our folklore is incorrect.

Wirt: Adrian and Scoble have raised the difficulty
of generalizing from local power conditions to the
elitist or pluralist condition of the national system.
My mind, however, goes to the reverse question. What is
the impact of the national system upon local power combinations? Walton has written convincingly of this "vertical axis," of transcommunity forces operating to frag-
ment elite, monolithic, or club-like regimes on the local
scene. To use Lowi's policy categories, such a vertical
axis cannot help but increase in the form of federally
funded policies of regulation (as in civil rights laws in
a Mississippi county) or redistribution (as in poverty
programs). What are the consequences for already established power structures, whether elite, pluralistic or
amorphous?

In Oakland, where poverty funds are twice the size
of the entire city budget, there's a grand scramble to
create structures to handle such money. New contenders
emerge in ghetto areas, and federal rules get injected
into the old game. The push by mayors throughout the
nation to change the law so they themselves can direct
the use of poverty funds is a clear sign that the present
law is upsetting old ways of using power to make decisions. Keep this up long enough, and you're bound to get
new local players and new combinations in decisionmaking.

Or in a Mississippi county where I've done field
research, new civil rights laws are having measurable
effects in restructuring the old power arrangements in

some decision areas, but not in others. Federal agents
have made the law's requirement to expand suffrage effective, and this introduces numerous new Black players into
state and local politics. Local office holders are
beginning to play the political game with them, simultaneously having to learn new ways to get votes by not
antagonizing whites. But in matters of job opportunities, the surplus unskilled labor doesn't match the few
jobs available, so federal law can't change local hiring
decisions too much.

All of this suggests a major research question:
What are the consequences of major national decisions for
local power systems?

Clark: Charles Adrian has talked about demand functions and welfare economics. Something called a social
welfare function has been discussed extensively by economists like Kenneth Arrow, and there has been a good deal
of disagreement on the possibilities of its measurement.
But measurement would seem to be essential before the
ideas we have been discussing could be used in empirical
research. Have you had any thoughts on the matter?

Adrian: I do have some thoughts about it. I commented that game theory was developed by economists and
econometricians in the early 1940's. Almost without
exception, economists now regard game theory as having
little explanatory value and as incapable of being opera-
tionalized. But I think that we have to grab at straws.
We shouldn't say that because game theory didn't work in
economics, it can't be applied to political science
effectively, at least for purposes of conceptual framework. You see, in economics, game theory didn't add anything to the conceptual framework, which was already well
established.

Further, this whole problem of measuring the use of
resources is very similar to the problem of measuring
statements concerning relative values in welfare economics. In all the years the welfare economists have

worked on this, they have not developed acceptable measures. So I think we probably can congratulate ourselves for beginning to move into some of the really tough central problems, those that are hard to solve. But I think that it would be premature to say whether or not we are going to be able to deal with the problem.

Clark: It is now time to open the discussion to the floor. Would anyone like to pose questions to either the panel as a whole or to individual panel members?

Question: You talked about the ideological commitments of individuals in the community in terms of power. What about the ideological commitments of social scientists in their research? Or are you speaking of ideological decisions that have to be made?

Scoble: That was the issue I was trying to raise. I'm saying quite frankly that when you get into this question of "Who benefits?" there is no "hard science" answer. You have to answer in terms of your own private values, and you can be more or less articulate about these. I'm being dogmatic and saying there can be no value-free political science, that ultimately we are involved in making very important value choices.

Question: What about those values in relation to the values of the power structure?

Scoble: You have a choice of selling out or being a nonconformist.

Adrian: No, you have a little more than that, Harry. Might as well get a little controversy going here. It does seem to me the problem is one step less acute than that. In general you can start by saying that you're going to look at the values of the alleged beneficiaries of a decision or program. Or you can look at the values of the deciders, those who agree to do something that allegedly will affect a particular problem. The serious problem that always arises is that you have to

decide what it is you are going to research. Of course,
in deciding to look at the value inputs of the power
structure, you may design the research so that you come
out with exactly the right kind of conclusion. That is
to say, the actors become heroes or villains in a self-
fulfilling prophecy. But I think that there are degrees
to which one's personal values control the results. This
is a question of professional ethics and honesty to a
degree. But ultimately, of course, the investigation
does depend on the researcher's values, just as it does
in physics and chemistry, although the area of discussion
there is very small.

Question: Dr. Scoble, you mentioned Domhoff's book
Who Rules America? What validity do you think that has?

Scoble: I have only read reviews of *Who Rules
America?* I did read the lengthy paper that Domhoff wrote
recently, "Who Made Foreign Policy 1945-1963?" Until I
see political scientists refute it--and I'm sure Nelson
Polsby will be around shortly to do this--I think it's a
pretty good study. But as I recall, Polsby has already
given his view on Domhoff's book. Didn't he review it?

Wirt: Yes. His review is coming out in the *Journal
of Politics.* It starts off with the line that "According
to Domhoff's analysis, I'm a member of the upper-middle
class. I feel like Groucho Marx who said that 'any country club that would want me as a member, I wouldn't want
to join.'"

Scoble: But however good the humor, it doesn't
necessarily answer the intellectual issue.

Wirt: I think his criticism is that Domhoff had
inferred the power to make decisions from certain class
characteristics, particularly economic and social-
cultural characteristics--the who-marries-whom type of
thing. And thus his critique would be much the same as
the one he made earlier of Baltzell's *Philadelphia
Gentleman.*

Scoble: Or the Protestant Establishment. But let me say that I think political scientists ignore social class variables at their own peril. In those four cities which Alford and I studied in Wisconsin, the whole structure of political action is biased in upper class directions. You're going to get certain kinds of policy consequences if this is so.

Wirt: How do you explain those occasions that arise all the time, where there are large numbers of people who have no resource but votes? They use their votes very rarely, but sometimes they get onto the scene and make a decision that overturns the Establishment's choice. How does this fit into your conceptual scheme?

Scoble: How often do they do this, empirically?

Wirt: Then we raise the further question, to what degree may not some kind of anticipated reaction set limits within which leaders operate?

Scoble: I think there probably is an important element of anticipated reaction. It's very hard to study specifically. It is just as important as what Schattschneider called the "mobilization of bias;" what Bachrach and Baratz are talking about in "The Two Faces of Power"[5] and "Decisions and Non-Decisions;"[6] and what we used to call "the climate of effective opinion" in public opinion courses 10 years ago. But it is exceedingly difficult to study. I'm willing to concede that.

Wirt: This is a central point for the "democratic elitists," those, like Dahl, who argue that we have an elite, but one which preserves democracy. They must postulate the conditions under which this anticipated

---

[5] Peter Bachrach and Morton S. Baratz, in *The American Political Science Review*, 56(4): 947-952 (1962).

[6] Bachrach and Baratz, in *The American Political Science Review*, 57(3): 632-642 (1963).

reaction effect actually takes place. This is important
for justifying their thesis of democratic elitism.

Comment: There is evidence that there is an anticipated reaction effect. However, the little evidence I've
seen indicates that politicians don't decide, "If we do
that, the people will vote us out of office, so we had
better be careful." Instead, they figure out a way to
act without risking electoral defeat, or they figure out
a way to rig the elections. There is a study of over 200
referenda in which the authors found that under certain
circumstances, people who feel powerless like to vote
"No." As a result, we get into very peculiar kinds of
fights over how to word the referendum so that voting
"No" actually means "Yes." That is, they figure out how
to do it despite the voters. But it is perfectly clear
from looking at political campaigns that the whole game
always is, and always has been, how to hold office without putting yourself in danger.

Scoble: How to get power without responsibility.

Comment: That's right, and so this anticipated
response does not mean that there is democracy. Far from
it.

Comment: This gets back to the problem of the real
values that are being distributed. You could say that
there is anticipated reaction; that, to some extent, the
political elite does not want to antagonize the public.
In that sense they are modifying their behavior to
satisfy the electorate. But unless you have some kind of
stable record of what the electorate really wants, then
what does the modification of behavior really mean? I
think Dahl could say we have a polyarchy because the
electorate, or the anticipated response of the electorate, does cause the politican to modify his behavior.

Scoble: Yes, but if that's so, why were the Blacks
so upset in New Haven the last four years? If Dahl was
right, shouldn't the system explain this? Or should the
system not produce this result?

Adrian: Well, let me introduce another variable, as if we don't have too many around now. The New Haven situation could be explained in many different ways, and I think one of the most probable explanations is a mistaken estimate of the political situation by the decisionmakers.

Comment: It is possible that there is modification of behavior, but is it the modification of behavior that the electorate really needs? Just how conscious is the electorate of its needs?

Adrian: This raises the question of the decisionmakers' willingness to expend resources, and it raises the question of their ability to "case" the job adequately. Serious mistakes are often made due to lack of knowledge and inaccurate analysis of situations that just can't be controlled. Or sometimes the cost of control is so high that a certain amount of hell-raising is allowed, because the marginal cost of avoiding it is just too great.

Comment: In your opening remarks, you said that communities were more open now. But in the Southwest, and the South particularly, we frequently deal with communities where the decision-making structure is not open, does not respond. In fact, it is pretty easy to find case after case where the decisionmakers simply don't respond to the community. Or else they seem to do something for the community, but there is no reaction. How do you make an analysis of this type, when there simply isn't the opening? I've been dealing with this myself for a year now, about 30 miles south of here.

Comment: I would like to comment on this question of the existence or nonexistence of political responses to social problems. One can best see social stratification in dichotomous terms: there are those who have and those who have not. But a recent study here shows that people rarely view their society in dichotomous terms, even though the ideological few assume that one can in

fact divide society into dichotomous parts. Perhaps this
explains how the populace votes on controversial issues.
They may say "Yes;" they may say "No." But they don't
have an image of what is good or bad, because they don't
see society in these terms.

Scoble: The Wisconsin data indicate that you are
right in suggesting that the average American does not
dichotomize the political world. Nor does he dichotomize
the social class world. If you ask people whether they
think of themselves in social class terms, they frequently deny it. Only if you press them rather hard do
they say, "Well, if I did have to apply a label to
myself, it would be this." And when you force them to
decide you find considerable misperception. Thus there
are many issues on which they don't clearly perceive what
values they might hold. If you asked these Wisconsin
people in 1962 what they saw as major local problems, 70
percent would see no problems.

Adrian: I think, too, that the typical citizen
often sees our political system as one with external
economies. In other words, he thinks, "Let George do it.
He'll do it pretty well, and he'll protect my basic
interests. I don't know what's going on, but I think
George does, and I'm not going to expend the resources
necessary to find out." In general, I think that Anthony
Downs's notion of information costs is very useful in
looking at community decisionmaking. By and large, the
typical citizen believes that it costs him a lot of
effort to find out a little bit, and this little bit
won't really change things. But of course he wouldn't
believe this if he didn't also believe that the system
is going to work out well in the long run.

Comment: This raises the question of whether man is
a political animal or not. What you were just saying,
Professor Adrian, is that most people don't act like
political animals. Dahl provides a great deal of evidence to support that. But I think it is interesting
and constructive to contrast Dahl's work with Schattschneider's. Schattschneider doesn't begin by pointing

out how little political activity there is, although he gets around to that. He starts out by defining politics, and he produces a remarkable chapter in which he talks about conflict being everywhere and touching everybody. So to Schattschneider the interesting question is not whether man is political. He is; all men are. The interesting question is: How has a system been built up which channels only certain kinds of concerns and interests into the formal political structure and leaves out others?

We often say that Negroes and lower status people aren't interested or educated enough to be "political." But they are political, as any white middle class man knows. But these attitudes and concerns aren't channeled into the formal political structure. There's no question that Schattschneider is right. There's no question that everyone is political. The interesting question is why only a certain kind of issue and concern is channeled into the formal structure of the political system.

Comment: You suggested before that the decision-making structure had little relationship to outputs. In the Dahl model, competition among elites creates responses. Now assume that decentralized decision-making structures exist. It would seem to suggest that if we can look at output in terms of responses (which isn't easy), then the result might undercut Dahl completely. Perhaps a pluralistic elite does not produce a more responsive output than does a monolithic elite. This seems to be one of the basic controversies in the whole power structure literature.

Scoble: I think you are right. Kaufman and Sayre's *Governing New York City* shows dramatically that a pluralism of elites does not necessarily mean competition among elites. You get what they call "mutual noninterference," very similar to what Lowi discussed in the 1964 *World Politics* article concerning....

Adrian: Conspiracies in restraint of trade.

Scoble: Yes.

Clark: That is precisely what we had predicted:
That a more decentralized decision-making structure would
make it harder to achieve the coalitions needed for decisive political action recorded in policy outputs. Some
findings on fluoridation and urban renewal by Gamson and
Hawley seem to support this interpretation. But we found
just the opposite: More decentralization leads to higher
outputs--at least in the form of budget and urban renewal
expenditures. It may be that with a highly fragile sort
of decision--such as fluoridation or urban renewal in
earlier years--a decentralized decision-making structure
leads to fragmentation and inability to decide. But if
the decisions are not quite so fragile--and it is seldom
the case that a community will allow itself to proceed
for too long without a budget--the larger number of
actors involved in decisionmaking seems to lead to continuing pressure to expand the budget and make greater
expenditures. As for urban renewal, it seems to be a
less fragile decision area now than it was a few years
ago. There is less ideological opposition, and many communities have already had experience with some form of
urban renewal program. The possible benefits of urban
renewal are recognized by increasing numbers of community
actors. Thus as more actors become involved in formulating a program, they are more likely to extend its benefits to the many groups involved, rather than ending in
total disagreement with no program at all, as seems to
have been the case often in earlier years.

Comment: We have said that pluralism doesn't necessarily invite competition among elites. I would also
argue that competition among elites doesn't affect the
output of the system. In fact, on the state level, when
socioeconomic development is controlled, differences in
party competition don't affect outputs very much.

Scoble: We are lost! This is the Dawson and Robinson kind of finding. Another cherished myth is destroyed!

Comment: No, I wondered if we could substantiate that on a local basis as well. Does competition have anything to do with outputs? Or do local parties simply argue about minor issues, such as whether there are hotels in town or not, whereas the real issues, the non-decisions, are never brought into the system and are never solved by the competing elites?

Clark: Is there anyone else who has some empirical findings that might shed further light on the relationships between centralization of decisionmaking and policy outputs?

Adrian: There are some findings that are relevant. Not only do we have the Dawson and Robinson article, but also the extensive work done by Thomas Dye, who shows that apportionment apparently explains some of the variance in output. But I'm inclined to think we haven't yet asked the right questions on this topic. The single most important factor, of course, is per capita income, but it explains only a relatively small part of the policy variance.

At the local level, perhaps we need to look at such aspects of governmental structure as the costs of achieving a decision, or the costs of putting something on the agenda, or getting or keeping it off. For example, Californians resort to a referendum on almost anything of any interest to the general public. This means that the rules of the game are very different from those in say, Connecticut. Perhaps a ruling elite could achieve the

----

[7]Richard E. Dawson and James A. Robinson, "Inter-Party Competition, Economic Variables, and Welfare Policies in the American States," *Journal of Politics*, 25(2): 265-289 (1963).

same thing in both states, but the costs of achieving it might be very different. So once again, I think we need to look more at cost benefit analysis.

Hunter: There is one other question of measurement that I would like to put to you. I wonder why we sociologists have been so reluctant to study ownership structures, the ownership establishment in America and community life? Who owns everything, and how does ownership change over time? This is hard to measure, but if we do want to measure progress this is one way to get at it. Basically, the goal of any given power structure is either to protect ownership structures or to gain access to them. This is what politics is all about. Within the next generation we could go out with pencils and paper and questionnaires and ask who owns what, and how the ownership pattern is shifting. But we don't really want to get down to the basic question, because there are a lot of people who don't want us to get right down to it.

[Ed. note: It seems appropriate that the colloquium, like this book, close with the remarks of Floyd Hunter. He is certain what community power studies would find, although pessimistic of our chances of making the studies. All participants agreed, however, that there is a need to continue such research. For we are still far from an inventory of community power systems in America, although the work of the NORC with its 51 communities represents an immense increase in available comparable data over that of even five years ago.

Pessimists and optimists, reputationalists and decisionalists, students of the case and the aggregate studies, political scientists and sociologists--all come together to continue asking the basic empirical questions about politics: Who has power and what difference does that possession mean for the lives of men? Implicit here, of course, is the normative question that has motivated such scholars from the time of Aristotle who put it clearly: "Our purpose is to consider what form of political community is best of all for those who are most able to realize their ideal of life." In the history of knowledge, this is not an unimportant task.]

Biographical Notes

CHARLES R. ADRIAN, Professor and former chairman of the Department of Political Science at Michigan State University, has been chairman of the Department of Political Science at the University of California at Riverside since 1966. He was administrative consultant to a number of Michigan state and local agencies, and to the Governor of that state. He is author or coauthor of eight books and several dozen articles.

CHARLES M. BONJEAN, Associate Professor of Sociology at the University of Texas, was editor of the December 1967 issue of *Southwestern Social Science Quarterly*, which was devoted to the subject of community politics.

TERRY N. CLARK, Assistant Professor of Sociology at the University of Chicago, is editor of *Community Structure and Decision-Making: Comparative Analyses*. The author of numerous articles on community power structure, he is a member of the NORC (National Opinion Research Center, University of Chicago) Permanent Community Sample Project.

FLOYD HUNTER has been president of Social Science Research and Development, a private research agency in Berkeley, California, since 1960. The author of more than 35 reports and papers, he is best known for *Community Power Structure*, *The Big Rich and The Little Rich* and *Top Leadership, USA*.

HARRY SCOBLE, Associate Professor of Political Science at the University of California at Los Angeles, is the author of *Ideology and Electoral Action*, as well as a well-known study of Bennington, Vermont. He is collaborating with sociologist Robert Alford on a study of leaders and nonleaders in four Wisconsin cities, and is examining the politics of regional economic development.

G. ROSS STEPHENS, Professor of Political Science at the University of Missouri in Kansas City, has produced a series of articles and reports based on field work in metropolitan St. Louis, Dayton and Kansas City. He is also author of a monograph on the metropolitan simulation model.

JOHN WALTON, Assistant Professor of Sociology at Northwestern University, is the author of a number of articles on community power, including "Differential Patterns of Community Power Structure: An Explanation Based on Interdependence," in the book edited by Terry Clark, as noted above. Most recently, Professor Walton has made comparative studies of political power and economic development in Latin America, with particular emphasis on Mexico and Colombia.

FREDERICK M. WIRT, Research Political Scientist at the Institute of Governmental Studies, University of California, Berkeley, has conducted community power studies in both rural and urban America. He is the author of *Politics of Southern Equality: Law and Social Change in a Mississippi County* (with foreword by Gunnar Myrdal). He has also written articles, and coedited with Willis D. Hawley a survey of the major literature of the field, *The Search for Community Power*.